THE BEST IN LIFE

Books by A. Lindsay Glegg include:

LIFE WITH A CAPITAL 'L'
YOUTH WITH A CAPITAL 'WHY'
CONQUERING THE CAPITAL 'I'
HOW TO RUN LIFE AT A PROFIT
FOUR SCORE . . . AND MORE
WALKING ON TWO FEET

THE BEST IN LIFE

SELECTIONS FROM THE MINISTRY
OF A. LINDSAY GLEGG

Chosen and edited by
JOHN L. FEAR

WORD BOOKS
LONDON

Published by Word Books, London,
a division of Word (UK) Ltd., Park Lane,
Hemel Hempstead, Hertfordshire.

ISBN 0 85009 042 3

First published September 1972

ACKNOWLEDGEMENTS:
Portrait by Grade
Quotations from The Living Bible by
permission of Coverdale House Publishers Ltd.

Made and printed in Great Britain by
Hunt Barnard Printing Ltd.,
Aylesbury, Bucks.

CONTENTS

FOREWORD

I am very indebted to John Fear for suggesting and compiling this book. The choosing of the extracts he has taken from my ministry, covering a period of fifty years and more, must have been an arduous task. He has had to read my six books and various addresses published in magazines, etc., and for this work alone he deserves a gold medal!

I have never found books of illustrations useful to me in my ministry, because stories taken out of their context do not have the same atmosphere, and also much depends on the way a story is told, which is difficult to translate into cold print. I hope this book will not suffer from this cause. I think John Fear has been skilful enough to bring in some of the atmosphere and application which clothe the illustrations and make them more effective.

I am more convinced than ever that the old saying is true. 'A bad speaker is one who has got to say something, but a good speaker is one who has got something to say.' I hope I may be included in the second category, for all that is in this book has first found its way into my own life and experience.

All that is of any value I owe to the goodness of God, and my heart's desire is to give Him all the glory.

A. LINDSAY GLEGG

INTRODUCTION

The provisional title for this book was *The Best of A. Lindsay Glegg* but as Mr Glegg's Ministry has spanned the entire Twentieth Century no-one could claim to have selected *the* best ten per cent out of the half million or so words from which this anthology has been compiled. I am indebted to Dr Paul S. Rees for suggesting this present title. As all of the published material has been out of print for some years I trust that this attempt to condense the rich heritage of Mr Glegg's ministry, into one volume, will provide a source of challenge and inspiration to a new generation of readers. The extracts have been arranged so that the teaching concerning the foundational truths of the Christian faith is progressive and care has been taken to see that they are consistent in meaning with the context from which the extracts are taken.

Lindsay Glegg's first book *Life with a Capital 'L'* appeared in 1934 and sold 100,000 copies. The Foreword began – 'Life is a great adventure'. This has been one of the keynotes of a life of high endeavour for God, splendidly maintained to a vigorous and fresh old age. His biographer, Dr J. D. Douglas, will record his adventurous leadership of many of the great evangelical enterprises of our era, but as one who has gained so much from Mr Glegg's encouragement and wise counsel I would like to pay this tribute during this month when he celebrates his ninetieth birthday. Lindsay Glegg has lived a busy life during the most eventful period in all history. He was nineteen when Queen Victoria died and as he recalls in *Four Score . . . and More* – 'At home my father kept a carriage and pair and we had three domestic servants to look after us, which was quite normal for the business man of those days' – so he tasted something of that period of ease and luxury. Living through the Boer war and two world wars Lindsay Glegg has been one of the most colourful and best loved personalities in the Christian world. Through shine and shade, grave and gay, triumph and trial, and amid changing and puzzling times, his life and character, gifts and graces, initiative and statesmanship has been an example to all who have been privileged to know him. 'Live so as to be missed' was the counsel of Robert Murray McCheyne, a counsel that Lindsay Glegg – or as some refer to him 'Mr Evangelism' – has been able to fulfil in a long and fruitful life.

Compiling this book has been a most enjoyable task – not least, because through it, I have been able to spend many stimulating hours with Lindsay and Netta Glegg in their gracious home 'Birchstone'. Mr Glegg has been full of suggestions and to hear him say – 'You must include an illustration about golf' (see page 134) or 'Did I say that? It's good!' has been reward indeed. The piece on Martha and Mary on page 100 was specially written for this book, because as Mr Glegg said, 'I wanted to say something nice about Martha.'

All the Biblical quotations, appearing at the beginning and end of the chapters, unless otherwise stated, are taken from the excellent paraphrase *The Living Bible* and I am grateful to Coverdale House Publishers Limited for their kind permission to do so.

JOHN L. FEAR,
Dawn Cottage,
South Nutfield,
Surrey.
JULY, 1972

Chapter 1

THE WAY TO GOD

Jesus said, 'I am the way, and the truth, and the life; no one comes to the Father, but by me.'
JOHN 14 *v*. 6 (RSV)

BE RECONCILED TO GOD:

The first word the New Testament has to say to any unregenerate man is 'be ye reconciled to God'. For our sin has estranged or alienated us from God, and our first need is to be forgiven and brought into fellowship with God. This is made possible by Christ's death upon the Cross. Many passages of Scripture make this clear – 'reconciled to God by the death of His Son'.

'Christ died for our sins.' 'He bore our sins in His own body on the tree.' 'He put away sin by the sacrifice of Himself.' So that when Christ died on the Cross, our sin was laid upon Him and He became our substitute and representative. Dying for us, in our stead, taking upon Himself the penalty and guilt of our sin. What a wonderful deliverance! Only God could have planned it and only Christ could have carried it out.

So I may know that my sins are forgiven and blotted out and that I am reconciled to God. Surely this is good news indeed!

Rev. Archibald Brown telling of his conversion says that on a certain Monday night he was under deep conviction of sin; on the Tuesday he was alternately swearing and praying; on Wednesday he was walking down a street I know well in South West London reading a booklet called 'The Sinner's Friend' when suddenly

the truth dawned upon him. He saw that Christ had died
for his sins and had endured the agony of the Cross to
bear those sins away for ever. He was so filled with joy
that throwing his hat into the air he shouted: 'Hallelujah!' He tells us that the first thing he did as a Christian
was to climb a tree to get his hat down!

Have you experienced the wonder and the joy of
knowing your sins are forgiven, of being reconciled to
God? This is the universal need of all men, not only for
prodigals and drunkards, but for the man 'who is doing
his best' (a strange term, for no man has ever yet con-
sistently done his best), yes, of every man.

*

How can I find God? How can I be reconciled to Him?
The answer is, by knowing the Scriptures and thus seeking
Him in the only way in which He can be found – that is
through Christ. It has been well said that there are a
thousand ways to Christ, but there is only one way to
God. There are as many paths to Christ as there are feet
to tread them, but there is only one way to God. Christ
said, 'I am the way . . . . no man cometh unto the Father
but by ME.' And again, 'I am the door, by ME if any
man enter in he shall be saved.' It is clear then that
Christ is the only One who can introduce us to and bring
about our reconciliation with God. And this He accom-
plishes by virtue of the fact that 'He died for our sins
and rose again according to the Scriptures.' For God
was in Christ reconciling the world to Himself.

REFORMATION IS NOT SALVATION

The history of our own country and of other lands ought to
teach us the futility of mere outward reformation. The
Puritans sought to sweep England clean and to garnish
it; they said in effect, 'We will make people good by
Acts of Parliament.' Certain public amusements were
forbidden; all Maypoles on Village Greens were cut

down. No one was admitted as a member of Parliament unless he professed 'godliness'. They cleaned up England for a time, but seven devils came in with the Restoration, and the Puritan era was followed by a wave of profanity, frivolity and immorality such as was never seen before, or has been seen since in our land. Literature reached its lowest level, and John Bunyan was sent to prison for preaching the Gospel.

The people of the United States of America tried a bold experiment when they went in for Prohibition, but noble as that action was, it brought with it an unprecedented wave of immorality, law-breaking, kidnapping and murder.

Far be it from me to decry the need for reforms today; there are a score of things I would alter if I could but let the message ring out again – reformation is not salvation, and the soul of man is never safe until Christ is received and enthroned.

SIN IS COSTLY:

Sin is always a costly business. Have you ever reckoned up the cost of disobedience? There is an old legend that a wise man once made a beautiful chessboard of squares embedded with jewels, and brought it to a king.

The king said: 'I will buy that board; how much do you want for it?'

The wise man replied, 'I want a grain of corn for the first square, two grains for the second square, four grains for the third square, and so on for the sixty-four squares.'

The king agreed to the price, and thought he had made a wonderful bargain – but let us reckon it out. All the cornfields of many kingdoms could not supply the corn to pay the price of that chessboard.

I once gave that illustration at my own Mission in Wandsworth, and the next evening a girl came to me and said, 'I have worked out the problem you mentioned: it has taken me all day! Here is the result,' and she unrolled a long strip of paper with figures stretching across it from end to end. I have no doubt she was right, for that enormous sum can be calculated; but nobody has ever reckoned up the cost of sin. What does it cost to disobey God? I cannot tell you ; it is beyond all human reckoning. To miss the will of God is tragedy indeed.

REPENTANCE – the gift of God

Repentance – it is a great word! May God give it back to the Church, that we may fearlessly declare it. What does it mean? It really means a *change of mind.* It means agreeing with God about things. It means having God's point of view.

I once had a conversation with a young fellow who seemed very concerned indeed. I opened the Bible and went from Scripture to Scripture with him ; and yet, somehow, he could not come to a decision; something held him back. It was getting very late, and when we parted I said, 'Now you go to your own room, and go over those passages again that we have read together and seek light upon them, and I will meet you tomorrow evening at 6.30 to know how you have got on.' The next night he was there at the appointed place before the appointed time – that was a good sign. And from his face I knew the question was settled; for there was a glow and a joy in his very countenance.

He said: 'It's all right: at two o'clock this morning I surrendered to Christ.'

'What kept you back?' I asked.

'Well', he replied, 'I am a bookseller, and I sell books, good, bad and indifferent – and I hand out every day to young people a great deal of literature which, if they read, will drag them down into hell.' I had a great battle to fight last night. I have got my living to make. But I thought over those Scriptures, and I marked them in red ink in my Bible. And it was two o'clock this morning when God changed my mind: and in a flash I saw

the horror of the thing I was doing, and I agreed with
God about it. And God gave me repentance, and Christ
came into my heart, and now the peace of God floods my
soul.'

                         *

Repentance is a gift from God. And there are Christians
who need that gift. Are we agreeing with God about
everything? God does not force us back into His will.
The father did not send a chariot into the far country and
bring back the Prodigal Son. The Prodigal Son had to
come to himself, he had to change his mind. He had to
see that his father was right and that he was wrong, and
then humbly to retrace his steps. And when he came back
of his own free will, having had a change of mind, there
was the kiss, and the robe, and the ring, and the shoes.
Do you need that gift? What about the way in which you
are spending your time? What about your business?
What about your pleasures? What about the books you
read? What about your friendships? Are you agreeing
with God about all these things? It may be that the first
thing you need is this gift from God.

SALVATION THROUGH FAITH IN CHRIST:

We should never have discovered the Way to God except
from the Bible. Human knowledge could never have dis-
cerned God's plan. But the moment we begin to read
our New Testament, we discover that salvation is *through
faith* in Jesus Christ. And what a discovery that is! It is
not intellectual assent, nor is it mere agreement with what
is written in the book, but a living vital faith in the Person
chat the book reveals. There is nothing in nature that
could have taught us the truth of 'salvation through
faith'. Human wisdom could never have devised such
a plan, but we learn from the Bible, and from it alone,
that this is the way to God.

                         *

When I was a boy, my father sometimes took me to the

Royal Institution where lectures are given on scientific subjects. I can remember a very eminent scientist speaking on some modern discovery, and in the course of his lecture he said, 'I have in front of me a bowl of molten lead into which you may plunge your hand and withdraw it again without being burnt.' The theory is that the moisture on the hand evaporates into steam and forms a kind of glove protecting the hand from actual contact with the molten metal. As a boy I was greatly struck by this remark and afterwards I walked on to the platform and peered into the molten lead. I believed all that the professor had said: I was sure that he was right. He had a string of letters after his name, and on such an occasion he must have been sure of his facts, but I don't mind telling you that as I stood there my hands were behind by back! There was plenty of intellectual assent; I would not have doubted the learned professor for worlds, but there was no faith. It is said of King Edward VII that when he was Prince of Wales he once heard a similar lecture, and coming forward afterwards he said, 'I am ready, Professor, here is my hand.' That is faith. That is taking the plunge. That is committing oneself. Faith is not merely believing what God has said, but venturing out on His Word, and acting on it.

*

There is a chemist's shop in America, which, it is claimed, has been open night and day for twenty-six years, and during that period a million prescriptions have been made up. The front windows of the shop are packed with the prescriptions, written on all kinds of paper and over the front entrance stands the slogan, 'Trusted a million times!' That is an effective advertisement; but it also carries with it a lesson in faith.

Think, for a moment, what happens when we are ill. We call in a doctor, and he writes out a prescription. We look at the hieroglyphics, and have no idea what they mean, yet we send down to the chemist and have the medicine made up, although it may be deadly poison for all we know to the contrary; and when it arrives we exercise perfect faith in swallowing it, according to the instructions.

Now, in the spiritual realm, this is just the kind of faith God is looking for: a faith that not only believes that His Son Jesus Christ is the Saviour of the world (that may be mere intellectual assent), but a faith that takes Him personally for salvation, and believes on His Name.

FORGIVENESS:

When I was a boy at a preparatory school we had a great headmaster; he had a wonderful influence on many of our lives. On New Year's eve he used to invite us all to a party. Out in the playground a bonfire was erected; it was so large that we used to have to warn the local fire brigade that when they saw the reflection in the sky it was not a house on fire it was only our bonfire! After we had tea, we gathered in the playground, put our hats and coats on and made a circle round this bonfire. Then the headmaster lit it, and the flames leaped up while we looked on in admiration and wonder. Then, when we turned round, we saw that the headmaster had gone. Presently he reappeared, carrying under his arm a book, a book that I soon recognised as the detention book – the book that our names were put in when we had not done our lessons, or when we had not behaved ourselves properly, a proceeding with which I was all too familiar! The headmaster brought out this book and our faces fell. Then he came into the circle, and the glow of the bonfire, and said to us, 'Boys, here is the record of your past misdeeds; here is your wrong-doing written in ink. This is the last day of the year; we are going to start the New Year afresh, and all the past is going to be forgiven and blotted out.' He took that great book and swayed it backwards and forwards until, with one great heave, he pitched it into the heart of the bonfire. How we cheered! We threw our hats into the air – one year I threw mine into the bonfire! – it was a great thing to know the past was blotted out. And this is the Christian's experience – 'the knowledge of salvation unto his people by the remission of their sins?' 'I will cast all their sins into the depths of the seas,' (Micah 7.19). That is quite as good as any bonfire, 'Their sins and iniquities will I remember no more' (Hebrews 8 v 12).

A FINISHED WORK:

'God sent His Son to be the propitiation for our sins.' We must begin there. The question of sin has to be dealt with. We first have to find our way to Calvary's Cross; it is there where our sins are forgiven; it is there where the great sacrifice for sin was made; it is there where Christ died and made atonement for us, according to the Scriptures. It is interesting to note that even God did not send Christ into the world primarily to be a philanthropist. Only twice do we read of Him feeding the multitude. Again, He did not come to be an orator. Our Lord brought to us no great perorations: His sermons were sublime talks addressed sometimes to only a handful of people. He did not even come to be a reformer. Does that sound rather strange? There were some great evils in the day that our Lord lived that He never denounced. Take, for example, slavery. I suppose it was the greatest curse of His day. It has been said that half the Roman Empire were slaves – there were possibly sixty million slaves living in appalling degradation, living lives that were nothing more than the lives of beasts. And yet as far as we know, our Lord never said anything about it. But our Lord did not come to be a reformer; He did not come to deal with the many social evils.

Then again, He did not come to be an educator. He left behind Him no writing of His own. We have only one record that He ever wrote anything, and then He wrote on the sands and the wind came and blew it away and left us no record of what He wrote. He came for one great reason, 'God sent His Son to be the propitiation for our sins.' He came to do a work on Calvary's Cross that no one else could do; and when He cried, 'It is finished' His life and His work were finished at the same moment, for in that hour He died for our sins. It was a finished work. The word, I believe, means 'It is rounded off to perfection.' That's it. He completed the work. In the Epistle to the Hebrews we read – 'When He had by Himself purged our sins, He sat down at the right hand of the majesty on high.' And again the same Epistle – 'This Man, after He had offered one sacrifice for sin for ever, sat down on the right hand of God.' When does a man sit down? When his work is finished. And the Lord Jesus had once for all completed His work; He had done what God sent Him into the world to do so that He was able to sit down at the right hand of God. The tabernacle with all its implements of service contained no seat. There was no place for the priest to sit down, his work was never finished, the sacrifice had to be repeated until the day came when Christ died for our sins once for all.

Having made clear the great purpose for which our Lord came to earth we must remember that after Pentecost the disciples went forth to teach, to educate, to reform until they 'turned the world upside down'.

JUSTIFICATION:

Once, when walking along Holborn, I looked up at the figure of Justice mounted on the top of the Old Bailey. The figure, as you may be aware, is blind-folded, carrying a sword in one hand and a pair of balances in the other. And I thought of the eternal justice of God. How could He be just and yet justify the ungodly? I looked again and there behind and above the figure of Justice, towered the dome of St. Paul's Cathedral, surmounted by the golden cross just catching the light of the setting sun.

And I saw there God's solution. The Cross of Christ provided the holy and effective ground upon which the sinner could meet God and be at peace. It is on this ground alone that we may draw nigh to God for salvation.

*

It has been well said that to create, God had only to speak, but to save, He had to suffer. He made man by His breath; He saved man by His blood. And on the Cross of Christ something happened. A mighty transaction took place between Christ and God. In the language of the Bible, 'The Lord hath laid on Him the iniquity of us all.' 'He bore our sins in His own body on the tree.' 'He was made a curse for us.' He took all the guilt, and the penalty, and the judgement of our sin upon Himself. He bore it all in order that we, who are united to Him by faith, might come out of condemnation, out of judgement, and stand in the place of forgiveness, and liberty, and life. What a wondrous message. Have you laid hold of this fact that –

> 'Bearing shame and scoffing rude,
> In my place condemned He stood.'

That is what happened. On the Cross He bore the curse of your sin and mine. He took the guilt; racial guilt, inherited guilt from Adam, personal guilt, my known sins and my unknown sins, all my sin from the cradle to the coffin. He took all that sin, and nailed it to the Cross, and, thank God, I bear it no more. I stand forgiven and justified in the sight of God. As far as the judgement for your sin is concerned, if you come to the Lord Jesus Christ now, and reckon on the merits of His Cross, and ask Him to be your Saviour, and to undertake the sin question for you, you may know that you are justified, with not a single sin laid to your charge.

The illustration of Captain Dreyfus has been given in this connection. You will remember how after his condemnation he was degraded in front of his own regiment. His sword was taken from him, the epaulettes were torn off his shoulders, his other decorations and badges were stripped off him, and then he was imprisoned on Devil's Island. Years afterwards, through the influence of some friends a new trial was granted, and ultimately he was pardoned and was set free. You might ask what more could he want, how wonderful that he was forgiven and liberated. But Captain Dreyfus was not satisfied, nor would you have been. He had been publicly degraded. The case was further enquired into, and this time he was acquitted and justified. Then in front of his old regiment, he was given back his sword, he was reinstated, and more than that he was given the rank in his regiment that he would have occupied had he never been condemned. It was reckoned that he had never left his regiment, he would have risen to the rank of Colonel, and, therefore, he was made a Colonel. That is justification: and God in His wonderful mercy puts us into that position, just as though we had never sinned.

ETERNAL LIFE – A free gift:

Apart from Christ, the Bible says, we are dead, dead to God; we cannot have fellowship with Him; we cannot commune with him; we cannot walk with Him, we are separated from God. As far as God is concerned we are dead. The world may look upon us and say that we are very much alive. It reminds me of a notice that was put up outside a churchyard in Ayrshire. They found that the graveyard was getting rather full; the dead were being brought from outlying districts and being buried there; and so they put up a notice, 'Nobody can be buried except the dead who are living in this parish.' It is quite true that there are a great number of people who think they are very much alive, but all the time they are dead to God. It may be true of some of you here. And you will never find your way to God until you come to Christ, Because

He is the Middle Man, He is the Mediator; He is the One Who brings us to God. And although 'the wages of sin is death' yet 'the gift of God is eternal life' because when you have Christ, you have life; and this life is God's gift. You cannot merit it; you cannot work for it; it is the gift of God.

Some years ago a man came into my office just about Christmas time, and he said he would like to make me a little gift; and he brought out from his pocket a very nice penknife; and handing it over to me he said 'Will you please accept this?' 'It looks a beauty,' I said. And the first blade I opened looked more like a minature bayonet. 'What's that for?' I asked. 'You clean your pipe with that', he said. 'That's not much good to me,' I replied, 'but it looks very nice'. Next I found there was a corkscrew. 'That's a bit out of my line too,' I said, but nevertheless there were some fine blades in it, and I put the penknife into my pocket, and I said, 'Thank you very much – it's a very nice gift.' Then my friend said, 'Would you mind giving me a halfpenny?' 'Why look here,' I said, 'if you like I'll buy the knife from you.' 'No,' he replied, 'I want it to be a present.' Then it dawned upon me that he was thinking about the old English superstition, that the gift of a knife cuts friendship so when I gave him a halfpenny, it no longer was a gift. However small the coin, I had paid him something for it, and therefore it was no longer a gift and our friendship would not be cut. That just illustrates what a gift is. Now if eternal life is a gift, you cannot do one single thing to earn it, or to merit it. If you offer God one good deed, if you offer Him one pious thought, if you offer Him one single bit of service, in exchange for eternal life, then it would no longer be a gift. The only way you can receive eternal life is by coming to the Lord Jesus Christ and saying,

> *'Nothing in my hand I bring,*
> *Simply to Thy Cross I cling.'*

We are not Godly; we are constant sinners and have been all our lives. Therefore your wrath is heavy on us. How can such as we be saved? We are all infected and impure with sin. When we put on our prized robes of righteousness we find they are but filthy rags.

ISAIAH 64 *v.* 5/6

I confess my sins; I am sorry for what I have done.

PSALM 38 *v.* 18

All have sinned; all fall short of God's glorious ideal; Yet now God declares us 'Not guilty' of offending Him if we trust in Jesus Christ, who in his kindness freely takes away our sins.

ROMANS 3 *v.* 23

I've blotted out your sins; they are gone like morning mist at noon! Oh, return to me, for I have paid the price to set you free.

ISAIAH 4 *v.* 22

Jesus said – 'I say emphatically that anyone who listens to my message and believes in God who sent me has eternal life, and will never be damned for his sins, but has already passed out of death into life.'

JOHN 5 *v.* 24

For God was in Christ, restoring the world to himself, no longer counting men's sins against them but blotting them out . . . . for God took the sinless Christ and poured into him our sins. Then, in exchange, he poured God's goodness into us!

2 CORINTHIANS 5 *v.* 19/21

There's a way back to God from the dark paths of sin; There's a door that is open and you may go in: At Calvary's cross is where you begin, When you come as a sinner to Jesus.

A Prayer of Commitment – 'Lord Jesus Christ, I admit that I have sinned and gone my own way. I am willing to turn from what I know is wrong, and I am willing to follow you and go wherever you lead. Thank you for dying on the Cross to bear away my sin. And now I come to You, Lord Jesus. I say 'I will'. I ask you to be my Saviour and Friend and Lord for ever. Thank you Lord Jesus. Amen.'

If you tell others with your own mouth that Jesus Christ is your Lord, and believe in your own heart that God has raised Him from the dead, you will be saved. For it is by believing in his heart that a man becomes right with God; and with his mouth he tells others of his faith, confirming his salvation. For the Scriptures tell us that no one believes in Christ will ever be disappointed . . . . Anyone who calls upon the name of the Lord will be saved.

ROMANS 10 *vs* 9/13

This Good News tells us that God makes us ready for heaven – makes us right in God's sight – when we put our faith and trust in Christ to save us. This is accomplished from start to finish by faith. As the Scripture says it, 'The man who finds life will find it through trusting God.'

ROMANS 1 *v.* 17

There is no other God but me – a just God and a Saviour – no not one! Let all the world look to me for salvation! For I am God and there is no other . . . . every knee in all the world shall bow to me, and every tongue shall swear allegiance to my name.

ISAIAH 45 *vs* 21/22

Chapter 2

NORMAL CHRISTIAN EXPERIENCE

Jesus said – 'I am the vine, you are the branches. Whoever lives in me and I in him shall produce a large crop of fruit. For apart from me you can't do a thing ... if you stay in me and obey my commands, you may ask any request you like, and it will be granted! my true disciples produce bountiful harvests. This brings great glory to My Father.'

JOHN 15 *vs* 5/8

Paul writes – 'This is what I have asked of God for you: that you will be encouraged and knit together by strong ties of love, and that you will have the rich experience of knowing Christ with real certainty and clear understanding.'

COLOSSIANS 2 *v* 2

Paul writes to the Christians at Ephesus – 'this is my prayer. That God, the God of our Lord Jesus Christ and the all-glorious Father, will give you spiritual wisdom and insight to know more of Him; that you may receive that inner illumination of the spirit which will make you realize how great is the hope to which He is calling you – the magnificence and splendour of the inheritance promised to Christians – and how tremendous is the power available to us who believe in God.'

EPHESIANS 1 *vs* 16/19
(J. B. Phillips)

Jesus said to His disciples – 'if any of you wants to be My follower, you must put aside your own pleasures

and shoulder your Cross, and follow Me closely. If
you insist on saving your life, you will lose it. Only
those who throw away their lives for My sake and for
the sake of the Good News will ever know what it
means really to live.'

MARK 8 *v* 34/35

'I'm glad I'm a Christian,
I'm trusting the Lord;
I rest on God's promise
Believing His Word.

The past is forgiven,
And now I am free,
A mansion in heaven,
Is waiting for me.'

ACCEPTANCE, ADOPTION and ASSURANCE:

Let it first be noted that the Christian experience is not
like a mathematical problem or a scientific treatise.
Science first considers the facts. If they indicate sufficient
proof, then the conclusion is accepted. Notice the order:
the proof comes first and the acceptance follows.

'Take nothing for granted', was the slogan my old
professor used in my college days. I can remember the
first experiment I had to carry out; it was to take sea
water, and by boiling off the water and testing the residue
that remained, to prove that the water had indeed come
from the sea. I was prepared to take the professor's word
for it that it was sea water, but that would have been
unscientific. The order of Science is – first the test, the
examination; and then, when the problem is proved, the
acceptance follows. Now the Christian experience is
exactly the reverse. God is not setting before you a mathematical or scientific problem. He is calling for *faith* and
the outcome of faith is the proof and experience which
follow.

We first come as sinners who are helpless and hopeless apart from the mercy of God. We find that mercy at Calvary's Cross and there we are forgiven, redeemed and born again.

The Christian order is first acceptance, then adoption and then assurance. First we accept Christ, and in accepting Him we are born again. Then God adopts us into His family. Someone may say, 'Why do we need to be adopted when we are born again into God's family? If I am a child, why adopt me?' A friend of mine, some years ago was presented with his first child. The doctor said to him: 'Here is your son, take him into your arms and adopt him.' But my friend argued, he said, 'If he is my child, why should I adopt him?' and the doctor replied, 'Go and read your Bible and you will find out.'

We are first born into the family of God, and then He adopts us, that is, He declares to all the hosts of heaven and earth that we are His. He owns us; He makes manifest that we are His sons.

Here then is the order, first acceptance, then adoption and then assurance – 'The Spirit itself (having come into our hearts when we were born again) beareth witness with our spirit that we are the children of God.

NO RECORD OF A BELIEVER'S SIN IN HEAVEN:

A friend of mine a year or two before the war told me that his uncle went to France for a holiday; he took his Rolls-Royce car with him, and was having a delightful holiday. He was nearing Paris when, unfortunately, he met with an accident, for some mysterious reason his back axle broke. 'That's finished my holiday,' he thought to himself. His chauffeur went to Paris and phoned across to the Rolls Royce Company and told them about the mishap. They at once chartered an aeroplane put a couple of mechanics on board with a new back axle; they flew over to Paris, and in a few hours they got down to the job, and fitted a new back axle. Soon my friend's uncle was on his way to the South of France enjoying his holiday almost on scheduled time. When he got home he thought he would write to the Company and congratulate them on their smart work. And as he was writing the letter the thought came into his mind – 'Let me see, who is it that pays the bill for this?' (That's something that makes a special appeal to me as one coming from Aberdeen!) So he wrote asking about the account.

Now, as an engineer who sometimes has got into difficulties, and has known machinery breaking down before now, I was interested in the reply of the Rolls-Royce Company. Their reply ran something like this:

'Dear Sir – Thank you for your letter. There is no account to render. We have searched the books of our company containing our records for years past, and we can find no note of one of our back axles ever having broken!' Mind you, they might break every week for all I know, but there is no record of it to be found in the books of the company.

When I heard that story I lifted up my heart and said, 'Hallelujah! In Heaven there is no record of my sin.' I am conscious of it myself, as the nearer I try to walk with God the more conscious I am of my sin.

Thank God, 'He put away sin by the sacrifice of Himself.' Now we are beginning to see something of the love of God for man. He gave His Son to die upon that cross, because there was no other way of dealing with sin – with your sin and with mine. But God sent down His Son from Heaven that He might in Christ reconcile the world unto Himself'.

ASSURANCE BASED ON THE WORD OF CHRIST:

Years ago during the American Civil War, it is said, there was a farmer's boy who was walking along the edge of a field, and he overheard General Lee, the commander of the Southern Army, say to one of his officers, 'I propose to attack at Gettysburg.' Now every one thought the Southern Army would attack at Harrisburg. That boy went home and told his father what he had heard, and the father telegraphed up to the Governor of Pennsylvania, and he sent a special engine down the line to collect that farmer's boy, so that he might stand and give evidence before their War Council. The Governor of Pennsylvania said to the boy, 'Did you hear General Lee say that he would attack at Gettysburg?' The boy answered, 'Yes, sir'. And the Governor of Pennsylvania said, 'I would give my right arm to know if that boy is speaking the truth.' It all hinged on the word of a boy. As all the world knows today, that boy was speaking the truth.

The great battle was fought at Gettysburg; the element of surprise had gone, and the victory was assured. Now, in the first instance, my assurance of salvation hinges on the Word of my Lord. Can He be trusted? Is His word true? Will He let me down? And the answer rings back from His own lips, as recorded to us in St. John's Gospel, when He says, 'I am the Truth'. My friend, will you venture out on His word? Will you receive Him into your heart by opening the door, and by reckoning upon it that He will come in – because you have His word for it; and you will enter into the assurance of salvation.

THE NORMAL CHRISTIAN LIFE

Life with a capital 'L' – the vertical line of the L represents the life in contact with God; the horizontal line, the life in contact with our fellowmen.

This, then, is the best life, the Christian life – life with a capital 'L'. Not simply a life shut up with God alone, forgetting the world around, such as some who live in convents or monasteries would have us believe. The vertical line by itself is the letter 'I' and represents a life that is

self-centred and egotistical. Nor is it a life that is spent
merely in social service – a life that leaves God out, and is
concerned only to serve mankind. That is the horizontal
line, which, by itself, represents a dash or a blank. But
life with a capital L is a combination of the two: first, the
life that is right with God; and then, as a consequence,
as an inevitable outcome, a life that is spent in serving
others. But let us put these things in their right order.
When we draw a capital L we start with the vertical line,
and then we make the horizontal stroke. And so it is with
this best of all lives – the Christian life. The first essential
is contact with God – the matter of our relationship with
God is of supreme importance.

DISCIPLESHIP

Matthew continued to sit at the receipt of custom until
one day the Lord Jesus passed by. He always passes by
when there is a hungry soul in need. And what happened?
Christ spoke first. If any of us are to come into blessing
it must be because the Lord Jesus speaks to us. A mere
human voice is of no avail. If we are to enter into a life
that is really going to mean victory and power and liberty,
it will be because the Lord Jesus speaks to us.

Christ said a very simple word to this man. There was no
arguing, there was no reasoning. The Lord Jesus looked
at Matthew, and said, 'Follow me!' and Matthew, we are
told, 'left all, rose up and followed Him.'

In a flash, the decision was made, and Matthew left
everything: he turned his back on the old life once and for
all. He was not only intellectually converted; he was converted from head to foot!

*

To leave all and follow Christ is the biggest thing that a
living soul on this earth can do.

*

The world thinks it madness for one to be an out-and-out Christian, and it has always been so. There were three people in the New Testament who were called mad, and for three different reasons. Our Lord was called mad because He spoke of His Cross; Paul because he spoke of the Resurrection, and Rhoda because she believed God answered prayer. To believe these three is looked upon as madness by the world today.

POWER TO LIVE FOR CHRIST

Jesus came to reveal the Father. To be my Teacher and my Example, but to be far more. The strange paradox of Scripture is that Jesus Christ came into the world to live in order that He might die. Why was His human body broken on a cruel Cross?

Here I believe the greatest miracle the world has ever known was enacted. 'The Lord hath laid on Him the iniquity of us all.' I believe that the guilt, the penalty, and the judgment of my sin was borne by Christ. I believe I have only one plea to offer to God, and one passport to heaven, and that is that Christ died for my sins 'according to the Scriptures'. This brings me – to use Bible words – forgiveness, reconciliation, and redemption.

Although I am a layman, I believe I may, and can, go straight to the Bible and learn the truth for myself.

I rejoice in the assurance that my sins are forgiven, but I need more.

I need a power in my life to deliver me from sin.

I believe that Christ rose from the dead. I cannot believe that His disciples went everywhere preaching His resurrection, and in consequence suffering persecution and death, when all the time they knew they were declaring a myth. They had seen and spoken to the risen Christ.

*

When a needy soul comes in contact with the Saviour the result is a new life, but faith must be centred in Him, and in Him alone.

I remember when a boy at school saving up my pocket money; and I assure you it was not very much, for both my father and mother came from Aberdeen! People may smile, but I had a good upbringing, and I thank God for the Puritan blood that flows in my veins. I still love to hear my mother tell of how she kept the Sabbath – nobody was allowed to whistle, or even to hum a hymn, and the blinds were not drawn up on Sunday. You had to compose your soul for worship, and then go and hear a two-hour sermon. Those days passed, but there is no wonder that Scotland produced some mighty men of God. They learned the Truth, and they learned the value of worship, and knew the power of the Word of God.

I saved up my pocket money, and I put it in a bank. I had great faith in that bank; I was sure I had put my money in the safest place on earth. But one day I opened the newspaper and discovered that the bank had failed, and 'bang went sixpence!' I had great faith but it was of no avail, for it was centred in the wrong thing. The bank did not merit my confidence. It is faith in Christ, in the Divine Son of God, that brings salvation. He is worthy of our utmost confidence. He cannot fail. All these blessings are ours in Him. It is not the greatness, or the magnitude of our faith, it is the greatness and power of the Lord in whom our weak trembling faith is centred.

*

Many may recall the story of Murillo's masterpiece, which hangs in Seville Cathedral. It is one of the great paintings of the world, and practically priceless. There is nothing to compare with it. How did it come to be painted? The great artist was in a monastery, and one morning he was inspired to paint – it was an irresistible impulse. He called for canvas; but they had no artist's canvas in the monastery. They searched around, and at last brought him some rough brown canvas, little better than sacking. That was all they had, but the artist took it, rough and coarse as it was, and stretching it across a board, he painted on it a world masterpiece.

Some of our lives are rough and ugly material. Yet the Lord would paint His own likeness, not only on such lives, but in our souls. He would fill us with His own Spirit, so that we may go out and live lives that are Christ-like.

*

Life is so full, it may be of Christian activity and service, that many people have no time to be quiet and to listen. This may be a very real danger, for by doing things that are good we may be missing the thing that is best. If you are too busy to hear God speaking to you, then at any cost, drop the thing that you are doing and get a quiet time alone with the Lord and His Word, that you may hear His voice.

Older readers will recall the tragedy of the Titanic, that great ocean-going liner that started on her maiden voyage across the Atlantic, with many famous people on board. When in mid-ocean, she encountered a fog, but the captain, a man of long experience, did not slow down, for he was not aware of danger ahead. Some time later the thermometer began to fall, an indication that icebergs were in the vicinity, but still the vessel pressed on. Not very far away was a steamer, the Mesaba, whose wireless operator sent out a warning to the Titanic that there were dense masses of ice right ahead of her.

Though that message was received in the Titanic's wireless cabin, the wireless operator, for some unknown reason, never delivered the message to the officer on the bridge. One of the ship's officers who lived to tell the story, has stated, 'Had we been aware of danger lying ahead, the ship would at once have been slowed down.' It may be that the wireless operator was preoccupied sending out messages to New York, arranging parties, receptions, and business appointments for many of the passengers on board, and did not realise the urgency of the Mesaba's warning. Whatever the reason, we all know that within the hour or so the mighty vessel, the largest the world had seen up to that time, collided with a huge iceberg, and hundreds of men and women perished – all because of an unheeded warning!

There are many people today who are too busy to hear the Lord's voice; they are doing a thousand and one important things until Christ is crowded out of their lives, and when He knocks and speaks, His voice is not heard. The central letters in the word 'heart' spell 'ear'. There is an ear within our hearts. Our Lord often said, 'He that hath ears to hear, let him hear', as if He knew how easy it was for us to miss hearing His voice.

*

A young nephew of mine, a few months ago, went for his first solo flight in an aeroplane. When travelling over his own house he suddenly crashed. His father ran to the end of the garden and discovered to his surprise and dismay that the airman was his own son. The boy was terribly injured, but thanks to modern medical skill and attention, he is now strong and well again. The cause of the accident can be summed up in a sentence – he was flying too low. That is the trouble with many Christians, they are living at a low level of Christian experience, and sooner or later the crash comes.

*

Becoming a Christian does not mean that life is one long bank holiday, I like the story of the little girl who was asked what she would like to be when she grew up and she replied, 'Mummy, I'd like to be a missionary on furlough.' But there is no furlough in the Christian life, you can't take ten minutes off and settle a quarrel just as *you* want to. God wants you to live for Him 365 days in the year and another day thrown in when leap year comes round.

*

'How do you know He lives today?' a sceptic once asked a boy. 'Because I spent half an hour with Him this morning', came the reply. And the Christian life is a life of fellowship and friendship with the Living Lord, Who, while He trod this earth, promised us His Holy Spirit to be our Helper and Guide and our Comforter.

*

The trouble with a great many of us is that we have no time to think. There is such a rush in this world. We are so occupied with business, with social engagements, and even with Christian work, that God does not get a chance with us. Some of us need to learn to be quiet – to think things out.

ABIDING IN CHRIST:

This subject is a most vital one for the Christian for it concerns his union with Christ. There are three great illustrations in the New Testament describing this union; there is firstly the illustration of the Vine and the Branches, then that of the Bride and the Bridegroom, and finally the great illustration given in I Cor.xii of the Body, Christ being the Head, and the believers the different members of the body. If we look for a moment at this illustration we shall discover some fundamental things that are directly implied.

(1) The Life of Christ corresponds to the blood that keeps alive every member.

As long as the head lives the body lives also, so at once we have a picture of our eternal security in Christ. Billy

Dawson, a Methodist Preacher, was once walking down
a street in a Yorkshire town when he came across a half-
wit trying to rub the engraved name off a brass door plate.
Of course the harder he rubbed the blacker the name and
the brighter the brass. At once Billy saw the lesson and
marching on he sang:

> *'My name from the palms of His hands,*
> *Eternity cannot erase;*
> *Impressed on His heart it remains,*
> *In marks of indelible grace.*
>
> *Yes, I to the end shall endure,*
> *As sure as the earnest is given;*
> *More happy but not more secure,*
> *The souls of the blessed in Heaven.'*

The late Mr. Fegan was once preaching in the open-air
on a very favourite text of his, John 10.28, 'And I give
unto them eternal life; and they shall never perish neither
shall any man pluck them out of my hand.' And, as he
was speaking of the eternal security of all believers someone shouted out 'but you may slip through His fingers'.
'Impossible', cried Mr. Fegan, 'for I *am one* of His
fingers.' How true was the reply, for Christ is the Head
and we are the members, and as members of the body we
are eternally safe in Him.

(2) *All the power of the head is at the disposal of the
weakest member of the body.*

This hand of mine could paint beautiful pictures if I had
the brain of Millais or Rembrandt; the fact that I cannot
paint is not the fault of my hand, however clumsy it may
look, but the trouble lies with the brain which is not able
to control and guide the hand aright. To abide in Christ,
to be vitally united to Him, means that all the power of
the Risen Head, the Son of God, is at our disposal. To

abide in Christ means that the very life, wisdom and power of Christ become ours. It is not our struggling and striving, but Christ in us that makes victory possible. Just as the same life blood that flows through the head also flows through each member of the body, so the very life of Christ flows out to each believer.

The Christian life then no longer becomes a life of imitation but a life of reproduction, not the life that seems merely a high ideal that it cannot attain to, but a life yielded to the Will of God, a life in which the Lord Jesus Christ dwells by His Spirit, a life in which, in a very real sense, He reproduces His own life. This seems a tremendous statement to make, but remember that life is made up of moments and as you abide in Christ, so moment by moment He abides in you. Open your heart to Him now and if He can keep you for this moment, He can keep you for every moment, for remember that 'a succession of holy moments makes a holy life'.

(3) *Notice the sympathy between the head and each member.*

If you pinch your finger it telegraphs at once the injury to the brain. What a sweet unity and sympathy there is throughout the whole body!

Now the moment you are face to face with temptation, the moment you are up against persecution, the moment you are in difficulty, trial, sorrow or loss, the Lord Jesus is instantly aware of it and there is a bond of sympathy between you and Him.

> '*Never a trial that He does not share*
> *Never a burden that He does not bear.*'

This wonderful link between Christ and ourselves always assures us of His loving sympathy in our daily lives.

(4) There is a vital relationship between the members of the body.

The same life pulsates through all, uniting us to Christ and uniting us to one another. This relationship is a closer one than even the family relationship. I do not know if family relationship continues after this life but I do know that those who are born again and are united together in Christ are brothers and sisters throughout all eternity. This is a closer tie than any human bond, let us thank God for it and love one another as those that are united in the Lord.

(5) Each member has a work to do for the Head.

Not all the same work, the hands are not called upon to do the work of the feet. 'If the whole body were an eye where were the hearing'? (I Cor.xii.17) Read I Cor.xii and you will see that each member has a work to do for Christ the Head, and there must be no part of the body inactive. If you are to be healthy, and we are speaking of spiritual health at this Convention, then you must be wholeheartedly in the Lord's service, using the talents He has given you and fitting into the plan He has made for your life.

But someone is asking how all this is to be made actual in daily experience. Look for a moment then at John xv.5. 'He that abideth in Me and I in him the same bringeth forth much fruit.'

the condition   – 'He that abideth in Me'
the promise   – 'And I in him'
the result   – 'the same bringeth forth much fruit'

Notice first the condition. You and I must abide in Christ, that is our part – the human side. It means that you trust the Lord, that you open your whole heart to Him, and that you are willing in all things to do His will, to let Christ the living Head control you. It means that you begin the day with God, and that you go on with Him making it the very habit of your life to live along the line of His will.

Years ago my father bought a horse for a firm he was connected with; it was at the time when the L.C.C. were changing over from the horse drawn trams to the electric system, and they had hundreds of horses for sale, fine strong animals that had pulled the trams along the streets of London for many a mile. Horses were going cheap and it seemed a most opportune moment to buy. My father made his choice, agreed the price, and in due course the horse was harnessed to the delivery van which started out on its morning round. Everything went well until the main road was reached, but the moment the horse got its head between the tram lines it went straight on and you could not divert it off the lines for love nor money! The old habit of its life came out and rendered it useless for the purpose for which it was bought. I have never forgotten that incident, for I learnt that if our lives are to be useful and to 'bring forth much fruit', we must make it our daily habit to live along the line of God's will. 'With God all things are possible', that means of course that God can do anything and everything – but it means more, it means that when we are 'with God', alongside His will, in Him, all things are possible to us. We obey the conditions and He fulfils His promise 'I in Him' with the glorious result 'much fruit.'

Will you begin this life today? God gives us a glimpse of our Risen Lord, our Head, and helps us to lose ourselves in Him.

Years ago in the Royal Academy there was a picture that created considerable interest, it was a picture of a boy and girl standing in a London Park; the rain was pouring down but neither was conscious of their circumstances; they were looking into each other's face and they were lost to the world; her face was to him all his earth and sea and sky. Oh! that we might have such a vision of the Lord that we might lose ourselves in Him.

Chapter 3

DIVINE RESOURCES

'If God is on our side, who can ever be against us?'
ROMANS 8 *v* 31

'You have received the Holy Spirit and he lives within you, in your hearts, so that you don't need anyone to teach you what is right. For he teaches you all things, and He is the truth.'

I JOHN 2 *v* 27

'The power of the life-giving spirit – and this power is mine through Christ Jesus – has freed me from the vicious circle of sin and death'

ROMANS 8 *v* 2

'The Holy Spirit helps us with our daily problems and in our praying. For we don't even know that we should pray for, nor how to pray as we should; but the Holy Spirit prays for us with such feeling that it cannot be expressed in words.'

ROMANS 8 *v* 26

'The whole Bible was given to us by inspiration from God and is useful to teach us what is true and to make us realize what is wrong in our lives; it straightens us out and helps us do what is right'

II TIMOTHY 3 *v* 16

'The earnest prayer of a righteous man has great power and wonderful results'

JAMES 5 *v* 16

'Pray all the time. Ask God for anything in line with the Holy Spirit's wishes. Plead with Him, reminding Him of your needs, and keep praying earnestly for all Christians everywhere.'

EPHESIANS 6 *v* 18

We are sure of this, that God will listen to us whenever we ask Him for anything in line with His will. And if we really know He is listening when we talk to Him and make our requests, then we can be sure that He will answer us.

1 JOHN 5 *v* 14/15

Everything belongs to you! Paul, Apollos or Cephas; the world, life, death, the present or the future, every-thing is yours! for you belong to Christ, and Christ belongs to you!

1 CORINTHIANS 3 *v* 21/23 (J. B. Phillips)

One of Peter Marshall's prayers – 'Lord Jesus, Thou hast promised to give us the Holy Spirit if we are willing to open our hearts and let Him in. Make us willing now that things of eternal significance may begin to happen. We know deep down in our hearts that without Thy guidance we can do nothing, but with Thee we can do all things. Let us not be frightened by the problems that confront us, but rather give Thee thanks that Thou has matched us with this hour. May we resolve, God helping us, to be part of the answer, and not part of the problem. For Jesus' sake. Amen.'

DIVINE PROVISION

The story is told of a man who once booked his passage on a steamer to Florida. It cost him nearly all he had and being as he thought, a wise man, he laid out his money in provisions. He purchased bread and cheese, it was all he could afford, to see him through the journey. It was a meagre fare, but beggars cannot be choosers, and he made the best of the situation. But after a few days the bread became stale and the cheese mouldy, and, worse still, three times a day he inhaled appetizing odours from the kitchen which nearly drove him frantic. Finally, the day before the journey ended, he met a steward carrying a great plate of roast turkey.

The very sight of it made him reckless. 'See here', he cried, 'how much will a dinner like that cost?' 'Cost, sir,' replied the steward, 'why nothing, it's all paid for in your passage!'

And if someone says, 'What a silly story,' my reply is that I can tell you something far more foolish. There are Christians living on spiritual stale bread and mouldy cheese, when they might be enjoying roast turkey from heaven! It's all included in the passage. Then lay hold, why live below your privileges? Read the first chapter of the Epistle to the Ephesians and see what an inheritance is yours. Go through the New Testament and underline the promises and then lay hold of them.

*

When we open the door of our hearts, the Lord Jesus Christ comes in. Our Lord enters as a guest, and at once becomes the host. At the wedding-feast in Cana, our Lord was there as guest, and when the wine ran short, He said to the servants: 'Fill up the waterpots to the brim.' He has taken the position of host; He is telling the servants what to do; He is providing wine for the feast; He has taken command; He was invited as the guest, and He has become the host. Again, when the two on the road to Emmaus came to their home it would appear that He would have gone on, but they constrained Him and said: 'Abide with us'. And He came in. He was their guest. But look, He is breaking the bread; He is at the head of the table; He is asking the blessing. Invited in as a guest, He has become the host, He is in control.

To receive Christ then means to hand over the control

to Him, and there is no other way to enter into a real
Christian experience. If you want reality, if you desire
power, then you must on your part fulfil the simple conditions of the text, for God does not give power to men
and women except in and through Christ. God has given
all power to Christ and God gives Christ to men, and
in so far as you have Christ and have enthroned Him in
your heart, just so far you will have power. For, remember, you cannot have the *gifts* of Christ apart from
the *government* of Christ.

DIVINE POSSESSION

Suppose I want to be a great batsmen; how can I manage
it? I dress myself up in spotless flannels, with pads and
batting gloves complete, and as I walk up to the wicket,
the crowd say 'There goes a fine batsman, look at his
perfect equipment!' But when the first straight ball comes
along my bails are off, and I soon find myself walking
back to the pavilion with another 'duck' to mar my record.
It was all profession; it was all put on from the outside.
I posed as a great batsman but it did not work.

A mere profession of religion is no good; the formali-
ties of church observance will, in themselves, bring no
change of heart. Christianity is not a matter of phraseol-
ogy, however pious it may sound; it is not something
that is *added on* to life, like the reciting of a creed, or
formal attendance at church worship. The solution of the
problem is not found thus. But my opportunities of
becoming a cricketer are not yet exhausted, for I can
take lessons; I can go out and practise daily, and
by perseverance and effort seek to become a great
cricketer, but I can see little hope of success along that
line.

And so it is in the Christian experience: it is not a case
of trying to do one's best, of self-effort, or self-discipline.
The way into the 'real thing' is not by trying to save one-

self any more than I could hope, by diligence and practise, to become a fine batsman. 'Doing one's best' sounds
so excellent and reasonable that somebody says at once,
'But nobody can do more than his best?' Exactly! And
that is why we all need a Saviour just because doing our
best will never save us. It is a great thing to come to the
end of ourselves and to see our need for Someone to
undertake our case and see us through.

To carry the cricketing illustration further suppose
that I could by some miraculous power, place the great
cricketer, Jack Hobbs, within my heart! I would invite
him into my life and put him in control, and thus
equipped I would walk up to the wicket and face the
bowling. 'Remember,' I said, 'Jack Hobbs is within me,
and as the ball comes down the pitch, he watches it
through my eyes. My hands are holding the bat, but
Jack Hobbs is in command, and he guides my arms, and
controls my wrists, so that I hit the ball full and square
to the boundary. The next ball, in the same way, is perfectly played, and all the wiles of the bowler are defied,
and I score my first century.'

But, you will say, 'you cannot get Jack Hobbs inside
you.' No, and that is the reason why I will never be a
great cricketer. But to be a Christian a miracle has to
take place – Christ, by His Spirit, comes into the heart
of every true believer, and He comes in to take control
and defeat the wiles of the devil. He comes in *to do the
saving*. He takes possession of my thoughts so that I may
have 'the mind of Christ.' He enters my heart and fills
it with His love. He looks through my eyes, and gives me
a compassion for all who are bound by sin, and so makes
the 'real thing' not only possible but actual. This is how
the Apostle Paul put it: 'I live, yet not I, Christ liveth in
me.' Writing to Christians, he said, 'Ye are partakers of
the divine nature.' And in another place, 'Christ who is
our life.'

So that when Christ comes into our hearts we have a
new life, we are 'born again'.

THE HOLY SPIRIT

God's gifts always bring responsibility. A blessing is never for ourselves alone; it must always be shared, or passed on to others. There are many scriptures which illustrate this fact. Take for example our Lord's words, 'Ye shall receive power after that the Holy Ghost is come upon you' (Acts i.8.). What is to be the outcome of receiving the Holy Spirit? – 'And ye shall be witnesses unto me.' Thus, every time we have fellowship with our Lord, and come into living, vital touch with Him, we go out into the world with an added responsibility, laid upon us to pass on the good things we have received.

*

To be filled with the Spirit means to bring forth the fruit of the Spirit and this is within the reach of every believer. We may not have all the gifts but we have all the graces. Many of us will never be orators; we may never take a great place in the affairs of this world; we can never hope to be clever, BUT we may be, and we ought to be, pure, loving, peaceful and full of the joy of Heaven. For within us dwells the Holy Spirit like a well of water, satisfying, purifying and supplying our every need.

*

Suppose I come to you with a royal request to say that King George desires to stay at your house next week. I think that you would soon commence to make all the necessary arrangements. You would be tidying up your house, getting the best room ready, and trying to make your humble home a fitting place for royalty. I cannot imagine somebody saying: 'Oh, yes, the King is coming! Well he can have a room in my house when he comes. We have an attic upstairs. There are a few boxes in it, and a bit of lumber; but I will have that cleared out and a bed put in.' Would you treat our gracious King like that? I would like to pause here, so that we may have time to think. Is it true that some of us have put the Royal Guest, the Holy Spirit, into the attic of our hearts? If so, will you ask Him to come down from the attic and take possession of the whole house. If the King were to come into your home he would take control. You would not have to worry about the programme for the day. The King would see to that. He always plans the programme in every home into which he comes. And so it is with the Holy Spirit. We grieve Him unless we put Him in control.

I was talking to a friend a month or two ago, and he said: 'I want you to go out to Palestine with me. I am going to take a holiday out there. I have been out before, and I know the way; I know all the ropes. It is not going to be any trouble for you. I will take the tickets, and plan the whole journey, and see you right through. I will be your guide.' Well, I do not know if I will ever go, but I can picture it all. There is the guide. I do not have to sit in the train worrying as to what station I am to get out at; for there is my guide, and I am reckoning on him. I do not have to worry as to where the next meal is coming from, or what arrangements have to be made. No, he knows the way; he has been there before, and I am reckoning on my guide. When you take the Holy Spirit as your Guide, He will lead you into all truth. He will teach you all things. He is a Guide to rely on.

*

In the olden days when a castle had a well within its walls it was safe, but if the castle was dependent on an outside source of water supply, which an enemy could cut off, then the people within might easily perish. The Christian has 'within him a well of water' – no enemy in earth or hell can destroy him or cause him to surrender. The Christian is invincible if he will but draw on the living water, the Holy Spirit within him.

*

There is a difference between the reception and the

filling of the Holy Spirit. When at conversion you received Him, your body became the temple of the Holy Spirit; that is solemnly true of every Christian. Be careful how you treat the temple, take care what you do with that body of yours. But have you been *filled* with the Holy Spirit? Are you rejoicing in this definite experience which alone can empower you to live the Christian life in all its glory and fullness?

When the Holy Spirit possesses you, He takes control, He comes in to plan your life, to guide you into the way of truth, to convict you of sin, to point out to you where life is wrong, and to make you very sensitive about sin and wrong-doing and to give you victory.

Some years ago on my birthday my wife planned to give me a present. On the morning she said, 'I have had a certain thing made for you, it is finished but I am sorry to say it has not yet arrived.' Of course I thanked her very much for it although I had not received it. I simply exercised faith. I had not seen the gift, I only had her word for it that it was ready and would arrive any day, and that was quite enough for me. Now, will you exercise the same kind of faith? Will you open your heart to Him and then, knowing that God will be true to His word, will you trust Him to fill you with the Holy Spirit?

*

Some of us have been wondering why we have not been filled with the Holy Spirit, why we have not had all the joy and grace in our hearts that we thought would follow our surrender to God. We have sought to get rid of those things that we knew were wrong in our lives, and as far as we know, sin has been put away and yet we still find ourselves longing that the Spirit may come in wholly and possess our lives. My friend, the Spirit of God does dwell within your heart if you are Christian, having made your body His temple, but that Spirit can never flood your soul and fill your life unless there is a way out for Him to flow through. It may be that you have been

looking on the wrong side. You have had your eyes
turned towards the Lord – that is good. You have put
away hindrances, as far as you know and that is good.
But what about the contact of your life with others? Are
you ready that the Spirit of God should not only fill and
flood your soul but that He, through you, should reach
out to others?

THE BIBLE

The Bible claims to be a unique book, essentially different
from any other book that has ever been written. When we
read the Bible we are getting into touch with the thoughts
of God, and we are enabling God to speak to us. If this
claim be true, and if all Scripture be inspired by God, how
necessary it is that we should read it and study it. What
folly it is to neglect the one book in which God had given
us a revelation of Himself. If we are to be strong, happy
and useful Christians, we must study the Bible. There is
a story told of a colporteur, who sold Bibles in the street,
and carried them round on a hand cart on which he
placed a placard with these words:

> 'The devil trembles when he sees
> Bibles sold as cheap as these'

And no wonder, for the Bible is the sword of the Spirit.
The Old Testament was the Word of God which our
Lord Himself used as His one weapon in the temptation
in the wilderness.

*

Dr A. T. Pierson has said, 'While other books inform,
and some few reform, this one book transforms.' And
the Bible today is transforming the lives of men and
women as nothing else can. It is carrying light and salvation wherever its message is made known. It has been

burnt in a thousand fires, attacked from every quarter, ridiculed and criticised, but it remains today the impregnable Word of God.

*

One of the miracles of the Bible is that within its pages lie the solutions of so many modern problems. It is the most up-to-date book in the world. It contains the answers to all our great questions, such as, 'Why did God make me?' 'What am I here for?' 'Whither am I going?'

*

A Christian has a textbook and an authority to which he can turn for guidance in all matters of faith, doctrine and conduct. I am so glad that we need not be confused and misled by the varying views of men; we may turn to Holy Scripture and find there God's plan of redemption, and His will for our lives.

*

PRAYER

A great many of us are praying, and we say we are leaving all the work to God and perhaps THE LORD NEEDS OUR CO-OPERATION.

Are we praying for the salvation of someone? Perhaps the Lord wants to answer that prayer through us. Is there a letter we can write? Is there a tract we can give to a friend? God may be waiting for us to act: or are we 'leaving it all to the Lord?' Of course, *we* cannot convert anyone; we cannot bring about the salvation of a soul; but we can present the truth, we can put the way of salvation before a soul, and the Lord may be waiting for us to do it. When sometimes we get down on our knees and pray for someone, is there not something left for us to do? It has been said that until we have prayed there is *nothing* to do; after we have prayed there is *everything* to do;

and God wants us to be ready to go out and allow Him, if He will, to answer our prayers through us.

Perhaps, one morning, we were praying very earnestly for someone we hardly ever meet, but we had a conviction that God wanted us to pray for that one. Then, while going through the routine of the day, we suddenly came across this person. Ought there not to have been a thrill running through our heart because God had brought us together?

*

There is a story told of a home where everything went wrong. Father was out of work; Mother was worried; when the biggest boy came home he was very cross. Nothing seemed to go right, and the little girl of the family looked on very perplexed. And that night as she got down to say her prayers, she said, 'Oh, Dear God, do take care of Yourself: for if anything should happen to You, what would happen to us!

*

It is not much good our praying for money to come in for a missionary society if we can go home and write out a cheque. It is no use praying for new workers unless we are prepared to go ourselves, if the Lord should call. We can pray through when we can say to the Lord, 'Here am I, use me.' God is willing and waiting to use a dedicated life that will, with great humility, co-operate with Him.

*

A man said to me one day: 'I cannot get up in the morning for my quiet time.' I replied: 'Unless you do get up early you will never be a soul-winner.' 'Well!' he said, 'I am not going to worry about it any longer, I am going to leave it all to the Lord.' I answered: 'I should not.'

'Why? I thought that would just suit *you*,' he replied. 'What would you do?' 'I should buy an alarm clock for five shillings. Why trouble the Lord about the matter? When the alarm goes off, just get up.'

CHRISTIAN FELLOWSHIP:

Henry Drummond summed it up years ago when he likened the Christian fellowship to a Club, the entrance fee of which is nothing, but the annual subscription is everything we possess.

*

Churches were not meant to be built up, but to be built out. The Church is not merely a happy centre for Christian worship, instruction and fellowship, but a centre from which people go forth into the world 'bearing precious seed'.

*

The New Testament never contemplates the conquest of the world by oratory. In the early Church they could not hold evangelistic meetings; the Church in those days was harassed and persecuted, and the Christians had to meet in caves and in hiding places. They only gathered in secret for their quiet times of worship and praise, and then, having received power from God, they went out into the world and by their witness, by their testimony, by the preaching of the Gospel, the Church of God was proclaimed on earth. And in three centuries even the Roman Empire had capitulated and Christianity spread like a flame of fire over the world. 'They went everywhere preaching the Word'. This could happen again if the Church became alive to its privileges and duties.

Chapter 4

CHRISTIAN CONFLICT & VICTORY

'No temptation has overtaken you that is not common to man. God is faithful, and he will not let you be tempted beyond your strength, but with the temptation will also provide the way of escape, that you may be able to endure it.'

1 CORINTHIANS 10 *v* 13 (RSV)

'The Lord is faithful; He will make you strong and guard you from satanic attacks of every kind.'

II THESSALONIANS 3 *v* 3

'No one who has become part of God's family makes a practice of sinning, for Christ, God's Son, holds Him securely and the devil cannot get his hands on Him.'

1 JOHN 5 *v* 18

'It seems to be a fact of life when I want to do what is right, I inevitably do what is wrong. I love to do God's will so far as my new nature is concerned; but there is something else deep within me, in my lower nature, that is at war with my mind and wins the fight and makes me a slave to the sin that is still within me. In my mind I want to be God's willing servant but instead I find myself still enslaved to sin. So you see how it is: my new life tells me to do right, but the old nature that is still inside me loves to sin. Oh, what a terrible predicament I'm in! Who will free me from my slavery to this deadly lower nature? Thank God! it has been done by Jesus Christ Our Lord. He has set me free.'

ROMANS 7 *vs* 21/25

'Your strength must come from the Lord's mighty power within you. Put on all God's armour so that you will be able to stand safe against all strategies and tricks of satan.'

EPHESIANS 6 *vs* 10/11

O Christ, our Saviour, the strength of the weak, the friend of sinners, and the comfort of the sorrowful: grant thy mighty protection to the tempted; reveal thy grace to the fallen; maintain the faith of those who are persecuted for righteousness' sake and give the consolation of Thy presence to all who are disappointed, embittered, lonely, or in despair; for Thy tender mercy's sake.

'Overwhelming victory is ours through Christ who loved us enough to die for us.'

ROMANS 8 *v* 37

'Be strong – not in yourselves but in the Lord, in the power of His boundless resource. Put on God's complete armour so that you can successfully resist all the devil's methods of attack. For our fight is not against any physical enemy: It is against organisations and powers that are spiritual. We are up against the unseen power that controls this dark world, and spiritual agents from the very headquarters of Evil. Therefore you must wear the whole armour of God that you may be able to resist evil in its day of power; and that even when you have fought to a standstill you may still stand your ground. Take your stand then with truth as your belt, righteousness your breastplate, the gospel of peace firmly on your feet, salvation as your helmet, and in your hand the sword of the Spirit, the word of God. Above all be sure you take faith as your shield, for it can quench every burning missile the enemy hurls at you. Pray at all times with every kind of spiritual prayer, keeping alert and persistent as you pray for all Christ's Men and Women.'

EPHESIANS 6 *vs* 10/18 (J. B. Phillips)

TEMPTATION:

When we take the Lord Jesus Christ as Master of our whole life, the devil will be at us with renewed energy, and we shall feel the force of temptation. Even Paul felt it. He said, 'When I would do good, evil is present with me' (Rom. 7.21). Then he went on to tell us the secret of deliverance: 'The law of the spirit of life in Christ Jesus hath made me free from the law of sin and death' (Rom. 8.2.). Although the law of 'sin and death' is still present, there is another law, another principle – it is the life of the Spirit of Christ within, which sets us free. Here is a magnet catching up some iron filings. What is happening to the law of gravitation? Is it not acting? Yes, it is still there; it has not ceased its pull; but there is a stronger force from above, and the filings have now come into that magnetic field, and each little iron filing is upheld by the power of the magnet which indwells it.

How can a Christian be free? By reason of *the life of Christ within*. Take another illustration. There is a bird flying in the air; how does it overcome the law of gravitation? By the life within. If that life ceases, the bird will drop like a stone to the ground. Here is a Christian; how is it that the world has no pull, the flesh is overcome, and the devil has no grip on that life? It is because of the life of Christ within mastering, dominating, possessing, and liberating.

*

Not only is God faithful, but He will not suffer you to be tempted above that ye are able. Well, that is good. You see, God is going to take care of you. He is not going 'to suffer you to be tempted above that ye are able'. He puts a hedge around you. That was the devil's complaint. You know how he wanted to get at Job, and you remember how he argued with God. He said, 'You have put a hedge about him; I cannot get at Job.' 'Take your hedge away,' said the devil to God, 'and let me get at Job, then I will show you what I can do.' The devil said a right and wise thing just then, and when the father of lies, for once in his life, speaks the truth, it is just as well that we should take notice of what he says. So God lowered the hedge a little and the devil reached over and he smote Job with boils. Then God lowered the hedge a bit more and the devil launched another attack, but God knows when the limit is reached. He has promised that He will 'not suffer you to be tempted above that ye are able.'

THE WORLD, THE FLESH & THE DEVIL:

There were two girls who became converted, and shortly after they were invited to some wordly amusement to which did not think their Lord would like them to go. It seemed to them to belong to the old life, and they had come out into the new life, and so they wrote a courteous letter. The duty of a Christian includes courtesy always! The girls replied: 'We are unable to come, because *we died last Tuesday week!*' They reckoned themselves dead to all that would displease their Lord, and they were right for that is the way of deliverance. That is saying no to self. The devil has no power over us if we are dead.

*

We who name the Name of Christ must depart from iniquity. Being re-born into the royal family, we must bear the stamp of the King. The world is looking on! Our life is open for all to see; and every time we fail the Lord, there is always someone looking on.

I was once at the Aldershot Tattoo. It was a wonderful sight to see the large amphitheatre nestling so naturally at the foot of the surrounding hills. Great searchlights lit up the whole arena as if it were day, and we watched the display and listened to the massed bands. Suddenly every eye was turned in another direction. A poor little rabbit

had got into the arena. There it was running for its life.
It was out of place – lost; and sixty thousand pairs of
eyes were fixed on it. The onlookers forgot for the while
all about the great display. I was only a few yards away
from Her Majesty the Queen, and I saw that she, too, was
eagerly watching the little rabbit. If you get out of place,
the world will be attentively watching you. If you are
somewhere where you ought not to be, every eye will be
on you. If there is something in your life that ought not to
be there the world will detect it.

*

How true the word is: 'Let him that thinketh he standeth
take heed lest he fall.' When I get a few days off in Scotland I am always happy to go fly fishing. Sometimes for
half an hour I will cast my fly across the surface of the
water, and nothing happens. I can picture the trout I am
after looking up at my fly, and saying, 'that's not a real
fly; I can see the hook and the rest of it is made of
feathers, and the wrong colour at that.' So I pull in my
line and try another fly, perhaps something more sombre
this time. And as I cast it over the water, the trout says:
'Ah this is a different story; here we have the real thing;
now for a wee bit of supper!' In a moment it is hooked,
and soon afterwards in my basket. The devil knows he
cannot tempt some people with the gilt and glamour and
tinsel of the world, so he waits his moment, he changes
his bait until he catches them on their weak spot. For he
has had thousands of years of experience, and he is subtle
and cunning and strong.

THE SECRET OF FREEDOM FROM THE
BONDAGE AND POWER OF SIN:

When I was a boy, my father took me to the Crystal
Palace to see the ascent of a balloon. It was a great thing
in those days for, unlike the present generation, we were

easily thrilled. We stood, my brother and I, in a large ring formed around the balloon which was filled with gas. It was tied down with cords all the way round, and in the centre one anchor cord. There was the balloon swaying to and fro and struggling to be free.

Presently the men who were to make the ascent came along and climbed into the basket. Provisions were put in, the necessary instruments, and sandbags round the outside. And as we two boys gazed spellbound, the man inside gave the signal that all was ready. Then an attendant with a sharp knife went round and cut the various cords, first this one, then the next, and the next, until there was the balloon swaying to and fro and held down only by the centre cord. Finally, amidst excitement, the last cord was cut; and the balloon was away. Forgiven, – washed; loosed – set free; that was the cry of the balloon as it soared into the sky, and that is what lies behind the word 'forgiven'.

There may be someone here who is saying: 'I would love to have all the cords that tie me to the earth cut, so that I might sail away into the skies, and never be troubled any more by sin and temptation.' But wait a minute. Let us get this thing right. When you come to Christ He does not pack you into a little bandbox and tie you up with pink ribbon, and label you for 'heaven', 'this side up with care'. No He sends you out into the thick of the battle. He has taken you out from the clutches of Satan. He has brought you out of the slave market of sin, to bestow upon you the freedom of His own service. And your old master is after you – of course he is. You say, 'How can I enjoy this freedom? How may I know liberty from the bondage of sin that has troubled me all the days of my life?

*

In 1916 there was a man in the French Army who overstayed his leave, and he was afraid to return to his regiment; he thought he would be had up as a deserter and shot. So his mother contrived to hide him in the attic of their home, and there, through the remaining years of the war, and through the subsequent years of peace, the man remained hidden in that attic. I suppose at night he would come down and walk the streets of Paris to get a little fresh air, but before daylight came he was back in his hiding-place. His mother fed him, and saw that he was clothed and kept warm. It was not until August 1st, 1937, that that man came out of his hiding-place. His mother had died, and there was no one to look after him and conceal him, and thus he was forced out into the streets of Paris. He went straight to the Police station and gave himself up.

The Police Officer said to him, 'Don't you know that when the Armistice was signed in 1918, there was a law passed which offered a free pardon to all deserters?' 'No,' said the man, 'I never heard of it.' 'Well,' said the officer, 'that law still stands; and if you care to put your claim in under that law, you are a free man.' And at once the deserter said, 'I claim my freedom,' and Louis de Court, for that was his name, belonging to the 10th class of the 51st Infantry walked out into the streets of Paris a free man. Why? Because he had claimed his freedom, based on a law that was bound to operate. Now, listen then to this: 'The law of the spirit of life in Christ Jesus hath made me free from the law of sin and death.' The devil will undoubtedly come with all his old temptations, and all the gaudy glitter of his wares, and present them to you. What are you to do? Look to your Lord and claim your freedom on the ground of His death and resurrection. He paid the price to liberate you from the bondage of Satan. Put in your claim. Send the devil about his business, for he is no longer your master. Someone came to me last night and said, 'How can I get over my impatience? I become irritable at business and it does not seem right, and it troubles me. I feel I am back again in bondage.'

Here is the remedy. Just look away to Christ, and claim the freedom that He purchased for you on Calvary's Cross. You will be tempted. The world will still tug at you. The devil will still be after you, but, remember, 'the law of the spirit of life in Christ Jesus has made you free from the law of sin and death.' The very life of your Risen Lord, the life that He gave on Calvary's Cross, and took again when He rose from the dead, that life is yours. And the liberty purchased by Him is yours. Claim it, and you will find that Christ will never let you down. His honour is at stake. Tell the devil that you have been liberated from his bondage and power, and walk out into life a free man.

'ON THE LORD'S SIDE':

You remember that Napoleon once took a great army and marched on Russia. And when he came to the city of Moscow, they set fire to it, and he had no alternative but to turn his army round, and lead it back as well as he could to Paris. Tens of thousands of men perished in the cold during that great retreat. Napoleon went to Marshal Ney, and said, 'You are in charge of the rearguard. Keep those Russian Cossacks back while I get the main army away.' The winter had set in, and the snow was falling. Those Frenchmen loved their Marshal, and they rallied round him, and in the cold nights as he lay down in his tent, they would slip in and lay their own overcoats over him. One morning when Marshal Ney went outside his tent, he saw standing there two sentries one on either side of the tent, frozen dead. They had no overcoats on! And when the men improvised bridges across the river, the engineers waded into the cold water and held up the parapets of the bridge for the army to go over, and as they stood there they were frozen to death. And as the Marshal passed over the bridge he pinned the Cross of the Legion of Honour of France on the dead men's breasts, One day in Paris there were four young officers seated at a table in a restaurant. And there appeared at the door, apparently, an old man; his clothes were torn and dusty, his back was bent, and as they looked at him standing in the doorway one of the young officers jumped to his feet and said, 'It is Marshal Ney,' and the other three sprang to the salute. They said to him, 'Marshal, tell us, where is the rearguard?' And the Marshal straightened his back, and lifted up his head, and said, 'I *am* the rearguard!' It was almost literally true. He alone was left. If men will own allegiance to a human leader like that, what is your allegiance worth to Jesus Christ? Are you coming out on His side? Will you join his great army? Will you make Him the Captain of your salvation? Will you say, 'Yes, I will stand for Him. I will unfurl the banner of His Cross. I am ready, He can count on me.'

SURRENDER – *The Secret of Victory:*

Fifty years ago a man crossed the Niagara Falls on a tight-rope. It was stretched across the falls from side to side, and he went over on foot. Not only was there the dizzy height, the noise of the Falls, and the spray around him, but there were very difficult wind pressures to negotiate: It was a very difficult feat. But not satisfied with that, he wanted to go one better. And he came to a young athlete, and said to him, 'I want to take you over on my shoulders on that tight-rope.' And the young fellow said: 'I have had no experience of these things.' But somehow or other that tight-rope walker inspired faith in that young man and he said, 'If you will tell me how, I will come with you'. The man said, 'The instructions are very simple. I am going to be the captain in this expedition. There is only going to be one mind at work, it is to be *my* mind. There is only one person in command, and I am going to be that person. I shall decide what shall be done at every issue, and you will just follow me. When I sway to the right you will sway to the right. When I sway to the left you will sway with me.

'When I lean forward you will just yield yourself to me,

and lean with me. At every point you will give yourself to me' And the young fellow said, 'I think I can do it.'

They started out on that great adventure, and they got three-parts of the way across the tight-rope. And then the long vibration of the wire rope broke in the centre into two, and each of these broke again into two and so on, according to the law of vibration, until the shortened wavelike movements became so violent that the tight-rope walker could scarcely keep his feet where he placed them. It was a very difficult moment, but the great expert handled the situation, and he swayed one way and then the other and the young fellow on his back just went with him. The master mind was at work, there was only one in control; and they were soon safely across on the other side.

Years afterwards, that young man at a Christian Endeavour meeting stood up to give his testimony. He said he had learned a great deal in that Christian Endeavour Society as together they had studied the Word of God; 'but', he said, 'I learned more about the way of victory in the half hour that I spent on the back of that tight-rope walker than I have ever learned since!'

*

I spent years *trying* to be a Christian. I did my best; I sought to obey the Commandments; I threw myself into church work; I repressed wrong feelings; I sought to smother my evil desires. And then one day I discovered that the secret was not 'repression' but *reproduction*. I found out that the Christian experience was only possible as I asked Christ to come into my heart and live out His life within me. I saw that I could not save myself, but that Christ would be my Saviour if I entrusted my life to Him and put Him in command. And I gave up struggling and striving, and I asked the Son of God to indwell me and keep me. May I say it reverently, I put the responsibility on Christ and I reckoned on Him. And I found I had a new life, a new power, a Saviour within me who could see me through to the end. The one condition is that there must be surrender on our part. I have heard people pray, 'O God give me more of Christ,' but you cannot have more of a person than the person Himself. The question is rather, does Christ possess all of you.

In Romans 12 *v* 1 the Apostle Paul appeals to the Christian reader to 'present your body to God'. That is a very practical thing to do, and my desire is that we might do it intelligently. 'But what is my body worth?' says somebody. If you ask a scientist, he will say that it is not worth much. An American has recently made a calculation. He assesses the value of the human body at sixty-three cents! He says that in our bodies there is enough fat to make seven bars of soap, enough iron to make a medium-sized nail; enough sugar to fill one shaker; and enough lime to whitewash a chicken coup – sixty-three cents in all!

But, tell me, what is the value of a body yielded to God? No scientist can reckon that up; no currency in the world can estimate the value of a human body indwelt by the Spirit of God. Your body is just the house in which you live; and if you present the house, you hand over all that is in it. It means not only yielding to God our hands and feet, but our hearts, and, what is perhaps the most difficult of all, our wills. To present one's body to God means to give all.

This will solve the problems of youth! A friend of mine some time ago was travelling to Southampton. He found a seat in an empty carriage at Waterloo, but just before the train started three young men came in. They made preparations for a game of cards, and invited my friend to join. 'No thank you,' was his reply. But they pressed him: they needed a fourth player, and he was just the man. They would play for money, but not for high stakes; why would he not be sociable and obliging?

My friend hardly knew how to reply until this answer flashed into his mind: 'I have no hands with which to play cards.' They looked at him in astonishment. 'What do you call those things?' they replied as they pointed to his rather large hands resting on his knees. 'Oh! those? They are not mine. There came a day in my life when I handed over my body to God, and those hands are His, and when I asked Him about it just now He said, No, His hands could not play cards for money.' So you see, the matter was soon settled.

Presenting your bodies also means the yielding of your feet. If some of us yielded our feet to God, they would carry us to China, or India, or Africa, to declare the Gospel to others.'

*

Here is a man suffering from asthma; there is plenty of air for him to breathe, but there is some obstruction and the air cannot freely get into his lungs. He does not cry, 'Give me more air', but rather, 'Let the obstruction be removed, that I may be filled with the air around me.' It is just the same with us in spiritual need. Christ takes what we give; if we give all, He takes all, and possessing us He saves us to the uttermost.

SATAN ALREADY DEFEATED

Satan has already been defeated, judged, and sentence has been passed upon him, and he knows it. The carrying out of his final doom is yet to come, but here is the description of it:

'And I saw an angel come down from heaven, having the key of the bottomless pit, and a great chain in his hand. And he laid hold on the dragon, that old serpent, which is the Devil, and Satan, and bound him a thousand years, and cast him into the bottomless pit, and shut him up, and set a seal upon him, that he should deceive the nations no more, till the thousand years should be fulfilled.'

Rev. 20:1–3

'And when the thousand years are expired, Satan shall be loosed out of his prison, and shall go out to deceive the nations . . . and the devil that deceived them was cast into the lake of fire and brimstone . . . and shall be tormented day and night for ever and ever.'

Rev. 20:7,8,10

So the story ends well for us, for our Arch-Enemy is to be cast into Hell, and it will only take *one* angel to bind him.

*

In every temptation, in every battle you have to face, there is a way of victory; and that way of victory is summed up in the one word – Jesus. 'Christ in you the hope of glory'. If you fail, it is not His fault, it is a hundred per cent your own fault. There is no reason why any temptation that may come upon you should get you down, because the Lord Jesus Christ, if you have accepted Him as your Saviour, has met Satan in open battle and has defeated him. He is Victor over the world, the flesh, and the devil. If you have received Him into your heart He is yours; His risen power is yours, power to conquer every foe that may ever face you.

Do you covet this victory? It is within your reach even now. On the strength of God's Word, on the strength of the testimony of millions of God's people down the ages, I can tell you that there is victory for you in Christ Jesus.

THE DEFEATED FOE

The physical body is not evil, there is nothing evil in these bodies of ours. Among the effects of James Russell Lowell, there was found a little tombstone with the inscription, 'Here lies that part of J.R.L. what hampered him from doing well.' That may be a pretty couplet, but it is not true. It was not J.R.L.'s body that hampered him from doing well, nor is it our body. Our body is to be the temple of the Holy Ghost; therefore let us take care of it. We must watch over our body; we must keep it clean, and strong, that it may be a fit house for God to dwell in,

It is not our literal flesh and blood that are evil. The Bible nowhere regards matter as evil. By 'the flesh' Paul means the sinful nature or disposition which uses the body as an instrument. Some who read this may say: 'This is not a very hopeful picture. The Lord has spoken to us and laid His hand upon things in our lives that are wrong. His searchlight has been turned on us, and we are feeling almost in despair, and are asking: 'Is there a way out?'

There is a picture that shows a youth sitting in front of a table on which is a chess-board, and opposite him is portrayed the devil. The devil is leaning back in his chair, with a leer of satisfaction. He has that young man in his grip; and there is a look of agony and despair on the young face. His hands are clutching at the arms of the chair, his muscles are tense, his face is drawn. Hopelessness is written on every feature, and underneath the picture is the word 'Check-mate!' A famous chess player who saw the picture called for a chess-board. He put the pieces in exactly the position that the artist had depicted, and then he studied it, and after a minute or two of careful thought, he sprung up from his chair with a great shout, exclaiming, 'The painter is wrong: there *is* a way out!'

Hallelujah! There is a way out. Christ is the way out. The devil with his leer of satisfaction, is a defeated foe. One day he is going to be put in chains. One day he will be cast into hell for ever. He is vanquished, and we may triumph gloriously over Satan and sin this very hour!

Chapter 5

SERVING CHRIST

'*The most important thing about a servant is that he does just what his master tells him to.*'

I CORINTHIANS 4 *v* 2

'*Everywhere we go we talk about Christ to all who will listen, warning them and teaching them as well as we know how. We want to be able to present each one to God, perfect because of what Christ has done for each of them.*'

COLOSSIANS 1 *v* 28

'*It is God's will that your good lives should silence those who foolishly condemn the Gospel without knowing what it can do for them, having never experienced its power.*'

I PETER 2 *v* 15

'*Dear brothers, warn those who are lazy and wild; comfort those who are frightened; take tender care of those who are weak; and be patient with everyone.*'

I THESSALONIANS 5 *v* 14

'*If we think that our present service for him is hard, just remember that some day we are going to sit with him and rule with him.*'

II TIMOTHY 2 *v* 12

'*Work hard so God can say to you, 'well done.' Be a good workman, one who does not need to be ashamed*

*when God examines your work. Know what His word
says and means.'*

II TIMOTHY 2 *v* 15

*'God has given each of us the ability to do certain
things well. So if God has given you the ability to
prophesy, then prophesy whenever you can – as often
as your faith is strong enough to receive a message
from God. If your gift is that of serving others, serve
them well. If you are a teacher, do a good job of teaching. If you are a preacher see to it that your sermons
are strong and helpful. If God has given you money, be
generous in helping others with it. If God has given
you administrative ability and put you in charge of
the work of others, take the responsibility seriously.
Those who offer comfort to the sorrowing should do
so with Christian cheer . . . . . never be lazy in your
work but serve the Lord enthusiastically . . . . . When
God's children are in need, you be the one to help them
out. And get into the habit of inviting guests home
for dinner or, if they need lodging, for the night.'*

ROMANS 12 *v* 6/13

'Do not be ashamed then of testifying to our Lord.'
2 CORINTHIANS 1 *v* 8

*'For we speak as messengers from God, trusted by Him
to tell the truth; we change His message not one bit to
suit the taste of those who hear it; for we serve God
alone, who examines our heart's deepest thoughts.'*
1 THESSALONIANS 2 *v* 4

'Lord, in the strength of grace,
With a glad heart and free,
Myself, my residue of days,
I consecrate to Thee.

Thy ransomed servant, I
Restore to Thee Thy own;
And, from this moment, live or die
To serve my God alone.'

Charles Wesley (1707-88)

FAITHFUL AND SUCCESSFUL:

We are sometimes inclined to say that God has called us
to be *faithful* servants and not successful servants. But
surely He has called us to be *both*, for our Lord said,
'Come ye after Me, and I will make you fishers of men.'
There is a great word in 1 Cor. 15. 58 for Christian
workers, 'For as much as ye know that your labour is
not in vain in the Lord.'

I remember finding this true at the most impossible
meeting I ever attended. I was away on holiday, and a
clergyman came to me and said, 'Will you help in an
open-air meeting? I have asked a Baptist minister to come
also, and he says he will.' I readily consented, and went
with another friend to the place appointed. There were
just four of us altogether, and not another soul in sight!
I remarked to the clergyman, 'Where are the people?' He
said, 'I think they will come along; anyhow we will begin
at once with singing. I have divided the town into sections
and this is the place for tonight, although I admit it is
rather lonely.' We sang a hymn – a quartette. Then we
had a word of prayer, and another hymn – the only two
quartettes in which I have ever sung!

After this, the Baptist minister mounted the chair and
gave us a clear Gospel message. Then the Vicar came
across to me and said, 'Will you give the closing word?'
I said, 'To whom, for I haven't seen a soul yet?' Nevertheless, as he was leading, it was my part to obey; so I
mounted the chair, and preached the Gospel as faithfully
as I could, and I never saw a soul other than my three
companions.

The next day, my friend was walking through the main
street, when a man came up to him and said, 'You were
in the open air last night, were you not?' He said, 'Yes,
but you were not there.' He replied, 'Oh yes I was – I
heard every word, and I wish I had had the courage to
come out boldly and listen. But I was hiding behind a
hedge. All the same I heard the message, and God spoke
to my soul.' So our labour was not in vain in the Lord.
Our work for God never is.

*

There will always be plenty of critics about who say 'To
what purpose is this waste?' How often has that been said
of some fine athlete who buries himself in the heart of
Africa, having left the field of sport to preach the Gospel
to the heathen? How often do the critics murmur when
some brilliant young doctor, with a 'future before him',
leaves home and friends and comfortable practice, to
serve God on the mission field in China or elsewhere?

How well it has been said that a boy on his knees in
prayer can see farther than a godless professor on tiptoe.
And these people who talk of waste know little or nothing
of the joy and privilege of serving God and of doing good.

*

Do you stand idle because you have not the hand of
Paganini or the pen of Shakespeare or Milton? You have
no voice like that of Caruso, but give God what you have
got. 'God hath chosen the weak things.' Why? 'That no
flesh should glory in His presence.'

Down the streets of Portsmouth over a hundred years
ago there walked a sailor; he only had one arm and one
eye, he was in a persistent state of nerves, unable to tread
a ship's deck without being sea-sick. If you had seen him
you would have said, 'He is just a case for the Home for
Incurables!' But his name was Horatio Nelson. The man's

spirit drove the flesh. How much more can the Spirit of God send us out in all our weakness to triumph in this hour? 'If God be for us, who can be against us?'

WITNESSING:

If we are really going to do business with God, there will be little time for reclining. Arm-chair Christians are getting us nowhere today. These are dark and difficult times. The churches are losing their hold on the majority of people in this country, the most favoured land in the world. I have been looking recently at statistics that have been compiled, giving the attendances at the churches in London, and the reading is tragic. We Christians have not yet awakened to the fact that we are not touching even the fringe of the masses for God. In London, great crowds are passing by our churches and our missions. The churches of London, on an average, are less than a quarter full. What a call to us all to get out into the highways and byways, and gather the prodigals in!

Have we made the conversion of others the passion of our lives? Many of us go out to business, and have to work hard there, but is the winning of others the *greatest* business for all of us? There is no time for reclining so long as there are prodigal sons!

*

A witness speaks of things he sees, but somebody may say, 'I was not with the Lord when He touched the eyes of the blind. I was not one of the favoured few that gathered with Him in the garden. I was not among those who stood around the Cross. I was never in the company of those that walked with Him on the road to Emmaus. What have I seen?'

Ask yourself: has prayer never been answered in your experience? Have you never had a vision of the Lord?

Do you know the joy of sins forgiven? If so, then go and tell others.

*

If there is one thing I would like to have said of me by those who are left behind when I have gone into the glory land, it would be just this – that the overflow hides the vessel! We may not know about it ourselves. 'Moses wist not that the skin of his face shone.' But the man working in the office with us is going to see something of Christ in our life. The girl friend of ours is going to see Christ in us.

Are we ready to let the overflow infilling us, reach out to others?

*

'There was a great revival going on in Antioch, and Barnabas was selected to go and see what it was all about, and he went to Antioch to make his report. What was it that impressed him when he came? Wonderful singing? No. Church members being enrolled by the hundred? No. Great enthusiasm? No. Great marches through the streets? No. 'When he had seen *the grace of God* he was glad' (Acts 11.23)–that is what he was looking for – 'the grace of God'. When you have led people to the Lord, and they have been truly converted, what you see is the grace of God. Such people have come out of prison; they have been set free; the chains of sin have been broken and the grace of God is manifested in their lives.

*

We are so often ashamed to speak about the Lord and there never will be a revival until God opens our lips and gives us such a mighty experience in our own souls that we must go out and tell others about it.

GOD'S MESSENGERS:

When King George was opening the Conference on Disarmament, a special room was prepared in New York so that the King's message might be relayed over the United States, But just at that critical moment an accident happened; a man crossing the room tripped over the cable and broke it. What was to be done? A certain Mr Vivian was in charge and he was almost in despair. To go and get his tools and effect a repair would mean at least twenty minutes' delay, and by that time it would be too late. Every second counted; there was not a moment to be lost. And he did what seemed to be the only possible thing that could be done – he threw himself into the breach. He seized one end of the cable in one hand, and the other end in the other, and there he stood as the King's message passed through his body, and went out over the United States.

For twenty minutes he stood there, and then when the speech was over, he fell, and they took him away to the hospital. God wants to broadcast His message through your body and through mine. The King of Glory has a message for this world, and He wants to send that message through human bodies. We have received His gifts, are we ready to let Him speak through us? God needs every one of us. We will never turn the world upside down until we humble ourselves before Him, and present our bodies to Him for this glad service.

POINTING OTHERS TO CHRIST:

Years ago, when my father was Mayor of Wandsworth, he presented a clock-tower to Clapham. There was only one condition attaching to the gift, that the Council were to be responsible for keeping the clock always pointing to the correct time. Whenever we passed by, we used to take out our watches to see if father's clock was all right!

But one morning, for some reason or the other, the clock stopped. After about ten minutes, it went on again, so for the remainder of the day it was ten minutes slow. Business men, hurrying across Clapham Common, looked up at the clock, and said, 'Hullo, we have plenty of time this morning; there is no need to hurry down to the Tube station.' Some talked together for a little while at the street corner, then, catching a train, found that they were late for business. Girls who served in shops and in offices came along, and looked up to the clock, 'Oh, we are in good time this morning; there is no hurry!' And, maybe, before they stepped on to the tram or bus they walked down the road and looked into the shop windows and selected a new hat or some such thing. They spent a little time in that way, and then went on to work and found that they were late! And there were boys who came along, going to school. They looked up at the clock, and said, 'We have plenty of time for the train,' and they sauntered down to Clapham Road Station, and they were late for school.

One clock pointed to the wrong hour, and there were many schoolboys late for school, men late at the office, girls late at the business house. 'What is your life?' Are you pointing to the right time? Is your life ringing true? You are a standard-bearer on whom the Lord is reckoning. Would it not be well if some of us thought in quietness about the strength of our unconscious influence? Is it counting for God?

CLEAN VESSELS:

D. L. Moody was very fond of saying, 'God does not ask for golden vessels nor even for silver vessels, but He must have *clean* vessels.' Is it necessary to press home this question? Are you clean? Are you washed in the Blood of the Lamb? That is where we must begin.

I was once speaking at a meeting with Dr Douglas

Brown. He told the story of Stanley Arnot, in a way that I suppose only he can tell it. He described how, when Arnot set out on pioneer work in Africa, he went into a new village that God had laid upon his heart.

Humanly speaking, the white man had little chance of returning alive from such a visit, so Arnot and his companions, before entering the village, knelt in prayer and committed themselves to God. They walked into the village, but nobody molested them, and in the centre of it they began to erect their tent. The little black boys and girls gathered round, and even crowded in to see what was happening, so Arnot had to make a roped ring in order that he could have a place to work in. But one little black fellow, with curly head and almost jet-black face, popped under the rope and came up alongside Arnot. He seized hold of the missionary's hand, and felt his fingers one by one, gazing at them in wonder. Then he looked up into the missionary's face and said: 'Sir, tell me the name of the river where you washed your black hands white?'

There is a hymn that modern people do not sing today, but some of us love it still:

> 'There is a fountain filled with blood
> Drawn from Immanuel's veins,
> And sinners plunged beneath that flood.
> Lose all their guilty stains.'

SERVICE FOR GOD IS COSTLY

Friends sometimes invite me to speak at their meetings, and they say, 'I know you are terribly busy but come and give an old address – it won't cost you anything.' I know they do it out of the kindness of their hearts, but if it doesn't cost me anything, it isn't worth anything. If God is going to bring something out of your service you must put your all into it.

THE NEED OF THE WORLD:

When our Lord saw the great multitude that had come out after Him, He saith unto Philip, 'whence shall we buy bread that these may eat?' In other words He said to Philip, '*add* up how much we shall need to feed this crowd.' And Philip did his best to sum up the situation and answered, 'two hundred pennyworth of bread.' It is to Philip's credit that he had an answer ready. I am not good enough at catering either to check his estimate or to offer one of my own!

Having got thus far, the next thing was to add up their resources, and here they discovered a lad who had 'five barley loaves and two small fishes.' The first essential in effective Christian service is to weigh up the need of the world – this poor world of ours, stumbling from one war into another, and living under the threat of the atomic bomb! The second thing is to sum up our resources; what have we got to meet this need?

THE CHRISTIAN'S TESTIMONY:

'Have you an up-to-date testimony? Have you a *present* experience of Christ's saving grace? Is he everything to you? Have you had answers to prayer today? I sometimes get tired of hearing testimonies to what happened twenty-five years ago. Let us bring our testimonies up to date. The thing that matters is, where do you and I stand *now*.

A story is told of an old man who had a wonderful experience twenty-five years ago, so wonderful that he wrote it all down and called it his 'Blessed Experience', and when people called on him he would often bring it out and read it through to them. One night, when a friend called in, he said to his wife, 'My dear, just run upstairs and bring down my "Blessed Experience" from the drawer in the bedroom.' She went upstairs to get it and on returning she said, 'I am sorry but the mice have been in the

drawer and have eaten up your "Blessed Experience"!'
And a good thing too! If you had a blessing twenty-five
years ago, and have not had one since, you had better
forget it, and get an up-to-date experience.

It needs the united testimony of every Christian to give
the world a full picture of Jesus Christ. Because each one
of us has a different, a unique experience of Christ's
saving grace: This is obviously so, seeing that we are
all different. Our temptations, our temperaments, our
circumstances, our very lives, are so varied that each of us
has, of necessity, a unique testimony to give. Give it, my
friend, and enrich the world by it. If we all went our way
to tell out what Christ is to us, I believe the world would
be startled, and multitudes would respond when they saw
the reality of the blessing that was ours.

*

The Rev. Archibald Brown used to be fond of telling a
story that he once heard from the lips of a seaman. The
sea breezes had kissed his brow so often that they had
left their mark there. And this old warrior of the sea when
he was asked where he found Christ, answered in a flash,
'Latitude 25N: Longitude 54W.' And Archibald Brown
said to him, 'You must tell me your story'. He said: 'I was
sitting on board deck reading one of Spurgeon's sermons,
and the light shone into my soul, and I took Christ as
my Saviour, and then I thought to myself, I will take my
bearing, so that I may know the very spot in the wide
ocean where I met with the Lord Jesus.'

*

When Lazarus was raised from the dead we read: 'By
reason of him (Lazarus) many of the Jews went away and
believed on Jesus.' We do not read that Lazarus preached
a sermon or indeed said anything. He simply had been
raised from the dead; he had received a new life from the
Saviour; he had been 'born again'. And the Jews came to
have a look at him and they found him a new creature,

and they were so impressed that they believed on Jesus, on the One who had given Lazarus life. It is not only the spoken word that God uses; sometimes our lives are more powerful than our words.

*

In my younger days we had to entertain ourselves; we had no wireless, no television, no gramophones, no saxophones and this applied to fashionable society gatherings. The following story is told and in its main details I believe it is true. A society party was being given in London's fashionable quarter – many famous people were there and each was asked to take some share in the evening's entertainment. The hostess approached a great actor, 'Will you please recite to us one of your famous pieces, perhaps a piece from Shakespeare?' The actor stepped on to the raised platform and to the surprise of everyone he recited the 23rd Psalm – his diction was perfect, every word was so beautifully spoken that when he finished the audience applauded enthusiastically. The hostess approached a clergyman and asked him, 'What are you going to do for us tonight?' He replied, 'I am not an entertainer I have no gifts in that direction.' But she replied, 'You could recite for us the 23rd Psalm,' and before he realised it she had announced him. With a prayer in his heart he recited the psalm. And when he had finished there was dead silence in the room broken only by the actor who stepped forward with outstretched hand as he said to the clergyman 'I know the Psalm but *you* know the Shepherd.'

Chapter 6

THE CHRISTIAN'S FUTURE HOPE

'And you are looking forward to the joys of heaven, and have been ever since the Gospel first was preached to you.'

COLOSSIANS 1 *v* 5

'I am comforted by this truth, that when we suffer and die for Christ it only means that we will begin living with Him in heaven.'

II TIMOTHY 2 *v* 11

'For this world is not our home; we are looking forward to our everlasting home in Heaven.'

HEBREWS 13 *v* 14

'Be patient and take courage, for the coming of the Lord is near.'

JAMES 5 *v* 8

'We are already God's children right now, and we can't even imagine what it is going to be like later on. But we do know this, that when He comes we will be like Him, as a result of seeing Him as He is.'

I JOHN 3 *v* 2

'For all creation is waiting, patiently and hopefully for that future day when God will resurrect His children. . . and even we Christians, although we have the Holy Spirit within us, as a foretaste of future glory, also groan to be relaxed from pain and suffering. We, too, wait anxiously for that day when God will give us our

full rights as His children, including the new bodies he has promised us – bodies that will never be sick again and will never die.'

ROMANS 8 *v* 19 and 23

Jesus said 'I go to prepare a place for you, that where I am you may be also.'

JOHN 14 *v* 2

'The Lord Himself will come down from Heaven with a mighty shout and with the soul-stirring cry of the archangel and the great trumpet-call of God. And the believers who are dead will be the first to rise to meet the Lord. Then we who are still alive and remain on the earth will be caught up with them in the clouds to meet the Lord in the air and remain with Him forever. So comfort and encourage each other with this news.'

1 THESSALONIANS 4 *vs* 16/17

'We live in the hope of eternal life because Christ rose again from the dead. And God has reserved for His children the priceless gift of eternal life; it is kept in Heaven for you, pure and undefiled, beyond the reach of change and decay. And God, in His mighty power, will make sure that you get there safely to receive it, because you are trusting Him. It will be yours in that coming last day for all to see. So be truly glad! There is a wonderful joy ahead, even though the going is rough for a while down here.'

1 PETER 1 *vs* 3/6

'O Lord, with our ears and hearts open,
Awaiting Thy shout would we be,
The summons that calls us to heaven,
For ever to be, Lord, with Thee.

Midst darkness, faith clearly sees beaming
The light of Thy coming afar;
We watch for the dawn of the morning,
And hail Thee, the bright Morning Star.

The word of Thy patience we're keeping,
Thy radiancy draws us apart–
A beacon us heav'nward attracting –
To meet Thee, the Hope of our heart!

D. Otsing, from the Russian

THE CHRISTIAN'S HOPE

It was a great day for me in 1905 when I came to Christ.
There is only to be one greater day – when I see Him.
When He comes again we are to be caught up – an act
of divine energy – taken by force. There is no law of
gravitation, there is no power on earth, that can retard
the uplifting power of God. It is a wonderful thing to look
forward to. 'He that hath this hope within him purifieth
himself.' (1 John 3.3.) If you are looking forward to the
coming of your Lord, I know you will be walking carefully before Him. If you know that any day He may
appear, you will be watchful of your life. My wife and I
are very fond of gardening. Some years ago, I entered our
garden for a competition arranged by one of the great
London daily newspapers. I went to our gardener and
said, 'I have filled up this form. We are going in for a
competition for the finest gardens in London. The judge
may come at any time. We do not know when; but you
will have to keep the weeds down.' Next morning, and
each time I went out to see him, I would say, 'What about
those weeds? Is the lawn nicely cut today? I wonder if
the judge will come today! Have you got the edges
straight? Are the plants tied up? What about that border
there; is that just as neat as ever it can be?' Each day we

waited in readiness for the judge. One day he came. Then later on, we had an illuminated certificate sent in as a reward for a garden of charm and beauty. I took it down to the gardener, and said, 'My friend, this is yours; frame it at home and keep it; it is your reward.'

*

Are there some weeds in your life? What about the garden of your heart? Is the lawn cut, are the edges straight and trim? Is that bed tidied up? The judge may come today – the Judge of all the earth, the Lord of Glory. Are you ready for His coming? We know not the hour when He shall appear but every day let us so live that if He should come we are ready to meet Him with joy.

OUR LORD'S RETURN –
A Comfort or a Craze?

Many centuries ago Horace laid down a principle for the guidance of those who wrote Drama which read something like this: 'No writer may introduce a god into the story unless the characters have got into such a mess that it takes a god to get them out of it.'

Today the world is a great stage and the people in it are the actors; surely we will all agree that they have got into such a state that only God can get them out of it. The world cannot solve its own problems, the solutions must lie with God.

This simple fact we seek to proclaim, that the wisdom and ability of man are utterly inadequate to deal with the situation, that man left to himself has always gone astray and always will. But the day is coming when God is going to intervene and Christ is coming again, first to take His people to glory and then to return with them and set up his reign on earth. Then and only then

EARTH'S PROBLEMS WILL BE SOLVED.

The question arises, is this truth a comfort or a craze? Some people suggest that as there have been so many cranks on the subject it is better to leave it alone. But there have been cranks on every truth, must we therefore reject all truth? There is not a doctrine in Scripture that cranks have not mishandled or a fundamental truth in Scripture that has not been twisted by well-meaning but misguided people. This is not surprising when we remember and recognise that the more 'out of the ordinary' a subject or a happening is – the more likely it is that all kinds of hasty impressions and unbalanced ideas may arise. All this makes the need more important and urgent for a clear statement on the greater truths of our faith and in particular on the truth of the Lord's return. This truth has suffered a burial like other truths before it. The great doctrine of justification by faith was buried until Luther resurrected it. The truth of sanctification was buried until Wesley resurrected it. And surely this is the hour when the glad tidings of a Saviour's return needs to be heralded forth with no uncertain sound. This testimony is based on Scripture, and the Second Advent truth stands second to none in the prominence given it in the New Testament. It is said that one verse in every 27 has reference to our Lord's Return (while one clear reference would settle it!), so that as we turn to the Book of Books

THE EVIDENCE IS OVERWHELMING.

It is clear that God must be ultimately victorious. The day MUST come when 'the knowledge of the glory of the Lord will cover the earth as the waters cover the sea.' Isaiah II.9. The last view that the world shall ever have of our Lord is obviously NOT as a malefactor hanging on a cross. THAT CANNOT BE THE END! He comes again to reign as King of Kings and Lord of Lords and His rule will be over the whole earth. It will be the day of His glory. The day of His final triumph.

To say that there are difficulties concerning our Lord's

Return detracts neither from the fact nor the glory of this truth. There are difficulties concerning all the great truths of our faith: who among us have fathomed the mysteries of the Incarnation, the Cross, the Resurrection? Surely the great fact that

OUR LORD CAME ONCE TO EARTH

and that to die, makes it easier for us to believe that He will come again to earth, and that to reign. The staggering thing is that the Son of God should ever have 'made Himself of no reputation', but having done so, it is natural for faith to look to Him to return one day in great power and glory. This indeed is the message of the Bible, stated in terms so clear and emphatic that they cannot be denied.

THE GREAT CLIMAX OF THIS AGE!

At the coronation of King George V and his Queen, many Americans and Canadians came over to London to see the great event. Their tickets included a seat to view the coronation procession, they were, however, greatly disappointed to discover that the seats allocated to them were on a barge on the banks of the Thames facing the Embankment wall over which they could see nothing. Many voices protested but the people were told to take refreshments in the rooms below and to wait patiently and all would be well. Meanwhile silently, but surely the tide was coming in and when ultimately the King drove past the barge was high above the wall and every eye could behold the Royal procession. We wait patiently for the coming of our King – we see Him not yet but the tide is coming in, and the waters are rising and we are lifting up our eyes in happy expectation: the signs our Lord told us to look for are being fulfilled in our midst and 'at any moment'

OUR KING MAY COME.

What a coronation that will be when our Lord will return to be manifested as evidently as to His disciples on the evening of His resurrection. This truth needs emphasising for many are saying our Lord is always coming to us – He comes first at our conversion and life is FULL of gracious visitations from Him who is the 'Lover of our souls'. This, of course, is gloriously true, but the Bible speaks of a day when 'This same Jesus shall so come in like manner as ye have seen Him go into heaven.' That certainly does not happen at conversion. The disciples saw the Lord with their eyes, they saw Him in His glorified body, they heard Him speak, as He said to them, 'Ye shall receive power after that the Holy Spirit is come upon you,' and then as they looked 'He was taken up and a cloud received Him out of their sight.' No language could be plainer than that used by the two angels when they said to the astonished disciples – 'This same Jesus shall so come in like manner' – *certainly* He has not yet come 'in like manner': it is an event to which we look forward, literally to be fulfilled according to

THE PROMISE OF HOLY SCRIPTURE.

To suggest that our Lord comes at death is equally misleading. If it were true we must re-write John 14: 'I go to prepare a place for you' as – 'DEATH will come and receive you unto itself'! And what can we do with such Scriptures as, 'The Lord HIMSELF shall descend from Heaven,' . . . . 'the dead in Christ shall rise first, then we which are alive and remain shall be caught up together with Him in the clouds to meet the Lord in the air'? There are some WHO WILL BE ALIVE when the Lord comes so that death cannot be the Second Advent for them; and as for those who are 'dead in Christ' – they also await the personal return of our Lord.

Once again, there are some who maintain that the Lord

fulfilled the promise of His coming at the destruction of Jerusalem in A.D. 70 but the book of Revelation, which deals so particularly with our Lord's Return and closes with the words – 'Surely, I come quickly, even so, Come Lord Jesus!' was written at least twenty years AFTER the fall of Jerusalem. If our Lord came in A.D. 70 neither history nor His own people have recorded the fact, and certainly those who were alive were NOT 'caught up to meet Him in the air'. The Italians were stirred in days gone by when men wrote on the pavements 'Garibaldi is coming'. And well may our hearts be stirred as we seek to write in letters of fire over all the darkness, distress and sin of the world 'Christ is coming!'

OUR HOPE IS IN HIM AND IN HIM ALONE.

The hope of Israel ALSO centres in His coming. Israel is to be restored to her own land.* What a troubled career the Jews have had, scattered today yet one day to be gathered together again! 'He that scattereth Israel will gather him,' Jer, 31.10. The only hope for this persecuted people is in the Return of their Lord to reign on the earth, when they shall see and accept the Lord Jesus Christ as their Messiah.

Once again, THE WHOLE WORLD ITSELF awaits this mighty Advent. The hour is drawing near when God shall intervene and the Lord Jesus shall descend from Heaven; first to gather His loved ones home, and THEN to return to earth with them to set up His Millenial Kingdom, – the Government of God – at last! The period *between* will be what the Bible calls the Great Tribulation, a time of unrestrained sin, and moral darkness without parallel in the world's history. In speaking of the reign of Christ upon the earth there are several points to be made clear. The first is that this reign of peace and righteousness cannot be brought about by human effort.

* This was written many years before the establishment of Israel as a nation—Ed.

The heart of unregenerate man is always evil. Civilisation and education may for periods restrain him but at heart man is still cruel, greedy, jealous and selfish. There is no stability regarding the plans that men may devise. It is clear that Christians will support wholeheartedly every righteous law and every good resolution whether it be a modified League of Nations or a system, whereby, for a time, peace may be secured but the Christian's hope cannot lie in these things.

He knows the unbroken record of human failure and he has a more sure hope. In the second place the true Christian does not look for the conversion of the world by the preaching of the Gospel. The Church's big task is certainly to PREACH THE GOSPEL and to witness to the end of the earth, but we have no guarantee, either from experience or from Scripture, that

THE WHOLE WORLD WILL BE CONVERTED TO CHRIST.

We are told indeed the very reverse, for 'evil men and seducers will wax worse and worse'. Already we see world dictators who foreshadow but fall short of the Anti-Christ who is yet to be revealed.

This does not deter us from preaching the Gospel; it is indeed a great incentive, for every soul that is born again hastens the day when His Church will be complete and the Lord will come. This is the day of Grace and the very circumstances of these days make the preaching of the Gospel AN URGENT NECESSITY. How long will this day of Grace last? How long shall the message ring forth 'whosoever will let him come'? At any moment God's clock may strike the hour and our Lord may come, and

THIS DAY OF GOD'S FAVOUR WILL END.

We read in Scripture of the Reign of Christ 'when all nations will be subject to His rule' so that we, who look

for the coming again of our Lord, are not pessimists but
super-optimists; we sing:

> '*JESUS shall reign where e'er the sun,*
> *Doth His successive journeys run*
> *His Kingdom stretch from shore to shore*
> *Till moons shall wax and wane no more.*'

We not only sing it, we BELIEVE IT, for the Scriptures
declare Christ 'must reign till he hath put all enemies
under His feet' and in that day 'every tongue shall confess
that Jesus Christ is Lord to the glory of God the Father.'
What a great day it will be for the world when God comes
down to earth in the person of His Son to set up His
reign of Righteousness and Peace.

> '*He comes to break oppression,*
> *To set the captive free*
> *To take away transgression*
> *And rule in equity.*'

So we are looking for

THE DAWN OF A NEW DAY

in the poor sin stricken world.

Dr Fullerton in one of his books tells the following two
incidents: On the extreme North of Norway lies the little
town of Vadso. There on the eighteenth of January each
year the people climb the hill and look toward the light
in the sky, and at noon the sun rises after months of night.
A little rim is seen above the horizon for a few minutes –
not more. But the people troop down the hillside glad at
heart. They know the long darkness is over, that the sun
will rise higher and stay longer tomorrow, and that SOON
it will be day even at midnight.

And away in the North of America at Dawson City,
where the river freezes in October and the last boat

hastens away lest it should be caught in winter's icy fingers, the people wait until May for their first touch of the outer world again. Across the frozen river they stretch a cord, which is attached to an alarm clock. When the first crack comes in the ice the bell rings, and, even if it is the middle of the night, the people rise and embrace each other, and laugh and sing and dance and feast, for they know that the thaw has begun and that

THE SPRING TIME IS COMING.

Next morning the world is still frozen, as in Norway it is still dark, but like ourselves they do not judge by sight. They have seen the light, they have heard the music of the bell, and THEY KNOW a new day will soon be ushered in.

THIS IS OUR FAITH – the world is at its midnight, but in the midst of all the darkness those who have ears to hear and eyes to see can hear the voice of prophecy and detect the coming dawn. 'Behold the Bridegroom cometh.'

We do not know the day or the hour. The late A. J. Gordon of Boston, said, 'There is a dogmatic certainty regarding the fact of Christ's coming, there is a dogmatic uncertainty regarding the time of His coming.'

But surely the day is drawing near; for every sign the Lord told us to look for, every circumstance which was to herald His approach is being literally fulfilled as never before. Watching the fulfilment of our Lord's words we hear again His exhortation – 'When ye see these things begin to come to pass, then look up, and lift up your heads for your redemption draweth nigh.'

And not least important is the fact that these truths are of the utmost practical value in determining Christian character and action. We are sometimes accused of having lost interest in the world, of being star gazers, of looking always for a coming event and forgetting the present hour. Well, it is always easy to criticise.

But there is more to be said. If the accusation is a serious one it must be answered, and the first reply is that all the great heroes of the past, the men who have really DONE THINGS FOR GOD have

BELIEVED IN THE SECOND ADVENT.

To tell their story would be like writing an up-to-date version of Hebrews 11. As we call the roll, Luther steps forward, followed by Wesley, Spurgeon and Moody. These great men certainly did things for God in their day. Wesley transformed the face of England; Spurgeon was a Prince of Preachers, and Moody's converts are found everywhere. But we must add such names as Müller and Dr Barnado who founded great orphanages and cared for thousands of orphans. Hudson Taylor and others like him founded great missionary enterprises in order that the Gospel might be broadcast everywhere. No, history is all against the man who declares that the people of this faith cut themselves off from the world and its troubles. Indeed, the reverse is true for an inspiring hope always stimulates effort and zeal. To have this hope is to be fortified, it is to see things in their right perspective; a man who understands a situation can always work better than a man who has no clear vision.

I can understand some liberal thinkers almost giving up. After nineteen hundred years of incessant preaching the world is still in chaos, whole nations cast God out and in spite of our education, our civilisation, our 'evolution', the world still cries 'we will not have this Man to reign over us.'

The modern preacher who seeks to convert the world must be disappointed indeed and the men who lose heart can never preach effectively.

But knowing the solution to the world's problems and knowing that the great day is near at hand, the man of Faith and Hope preaches and works as never before, for he knows the time is short and the hour is urgent and he must be found faithful and 'occupied' when his Lord comes.

It is helpful to note that the New Testament is full of exhortations to godliness based on the fact of our Lord's Return. 'And every man that hath this hope in him purifieth himself, even as He is pure.'

'Therefore, be ye also ready, for in such an hour as ye think not the Son of Man cometh.' And such words as these fell from the lips of our Lord: 'take heed to yourselves. Watch ye, therefore, and pray always,' and in every case reference is to

HIS RETURN.

When France declared war in 1870 it is said that Von Moltke was wakened at night and told of the fact. He said coolly to the official who roused him: 'Go to pigeon Hole No – in my safe, take a paper from it and telegraph as there directed to the different troops of the Empire.' He then turned over and went to sleep, and awoke at his accustomed hour in the morning. Everyone else in Berlin was very much excited, but Von Moltke took his morning walk as usual, and a friend who met him said: 'General you seem to be taking it very easy, aren't you afraid of the situation? I should think you would be very busy.' 'Ah,' replied Von Moltke, 'all my work for this time has been done beforehand and everything that can be done now has been done.'

He was ready. I wonder if we are ready, living each day in the knowledge that Christ may come? Resting each night in the happy assurance that the day's work is done – no sins unconfessed to our Lord, no grudge to our fellow-man remembered, no slander unforgiven. Ready for the higher call when we shall meet Him 'in the air'! Thank God, if we belong to Christ we are on the winning side. Thank God, there is victory ahead, – GOD'S OWN VICTORY!

THE LORD 'SHALL APPEAR A SECOND TIME'

and we who are His own shall be WITH HIM, and 'WE SHALL BE LIKE HIM: FOR WE SHALL SEE HIM AS HE IS'

(1. JOHN 3. 1–3)

Chapter 7

TRANSFORMED LIVES

'The same good news that came to you is going out all over the world and changing lives everywhere, just as it changed yours that very first day you heard it and understood about God's great kindness to sinners.'
COLOSSIANS 1 *v* 6

'Once you were less than nothing; now you are God's own. Once you knew very little of God's kindness; now your very lives have been changed by it.'
I PETER 2 *v* 10

'Amazing grace! how sweet the sound, That saved a wretch like me! I once was lost, but now am found. Was blind, but now I see.'
JOHN NEWTON (1725-1807)

'All who heard Paul were amazed. "Isn't this the same man who persecuted Jesus' followers so bitterly in Jerusalem?" They asked.'
ACTS 9 *v* 21

MATTHEW:

Some ask 'What is this life of following Christ going to mean? To what am I committing myself, for this is something of which I have but the vaguest idea?' Here are some of the things that it meant for Matthew. Luke, in his description of this incident, says, 'Levi made him a great feast in his own house' (Luke 5.29) But when Matthew writes about it, he says, 'And it came to pass, as

Jesus sat at meat in the house (Matt. 9.10). Matthew! –
you prepared the feast. It was your business, and in your
house, too. You sent out the invitations but you have left
your name out of it! Here is a man by nature boastful,
pushing, egotistical, a bully. But, now – what humility!
What a mighty change! Matthew: where is he? He is not
in the picture. He is concerned only with his Lord!

A TRANSFORMED PERSONALITY

It meant a big thing for Matthew, and it will mean a big
thing for all of us when we come into this blessing. Some
young people are saying, 'I do not want my personality
smothered. I do not want all the energy and go knocked
out of me.' The Lord does not destroy personality: He
transforms it. What did Matthew do? Before Christ came
his way, Matthew used to be a schemer. He had to make
his living by his wits: he had to get the taxes in somehow;
it did not matter how much he extorted.

But what do we see Matthew doing now? He is scheming still, but with a difference. He is scheming now for
God. He is thinking about his fellow publicans, and he is
saying, 'How can I get hold of them? What scheme can I
evolve? I will have a great feast; they will come to that!'
All the energy, zeal, and enthusiasm that he threw into
the old life are now given to Christ.

That is what it means to follow Christ. Matthew did
not cut himself off from his old companions. They were
on the road to destruction, and he was out to win them.

When you follow Christ you will get a heart of love
that takes in the whole world, and you will go down into
that world, for your Master will lead you there, and you
will begin to put all the energy with which you once
served the devil into Christ's holy service.

GEORGE MÜLLER:

A boy, born near Halberstadt, in Prussia, who grows up
to break his mother's heart. Even while she is dying, he is

playing cards and gambling. He roams the streets at night, half drunk, and eventually finds his way to prison as a thief and vagabond.

Now look for a moment at a city in the West of England. The cathedral flag is at half-mast, all shops are shut, thousands line the streets. Many people in tears.

Look at the procession; they are laying to rest the profligate and thief of Halberstadt! But what is the meaning of it all? It is, that there came a time when George Müller 'believed on the Name' of God's Son, Jesus Christ, and the result was that he was given such a big heart of love that he became a father to thousands of poor children and raised over two million pounds to keep them, without asking a penny.

THOMAS BRIDGES

The miracles wrought by this book (the bible) form the most thrilling stories in the pages of history. Here is but one tale to which ten thousand could be added: One day on the steps of St. Thomas's Hospital there lay what appeared to be a bundle of rags. It was picked up by a nurse, and within the rags she found a little baby boy. He seemed to belong to nobody, and nobody belonged to him; so he was taken into the hospital and cared for.

He was the pet of all the nurses but they did not know what to call him, so they named him Thomas, from the patron saint of the hospital, under whose roof he was nourished and cared for. But a boy must have two names, so they called him Bridges because of the two which span the Thames on either side of the hospital.

So Tom Bridges grew up to be a sturdy boy, and then into a fine looking young man. But best of all, he learnt to love his Bible, and to trust the Saviour, who is revealed therein.

It was about this time that the famous Charles Darwin returned from his visit to Tierra del Fuego, and reported that the people of that land were the most degraded and hopeless people in the world, and he declared, 'I would rather try to civilize the dogs in the streets than those people.' Tom Bridges heard what Darwin had said, and he thought to himself, 'I know what will uplift and civilize these people. I know of a Book that has transformed my life, and taught me of a Saviour who can save to the uttermost.' And God called him to this seemingly impossible task. He offered himself as a missionary to Tierra del Fuego and was accepted, and he went to live among the lowest humanity on the face of the earth. He had but one treasured possession – the Bible. It was the book that fitted him for God's service, and the weapon whereby he could slay the powers of darkness.

Twelve years after his first visit, Charles Darwin went again to Tierra del Fuego, and as he landed he heard a strange sound, it was the call to morning worship ringing out through the village; and as he looked, he saw little groups of men and women coming down the valleys to meet in the little chapel. Men clothed, possessing many of the comforts of civilization, and living in harmony, were gathering to hear the holy words of Scripture, and to worship the God of all grace.

God had used one man, with the love of Christ in his heart, and the Word of God in his hand, to bring about that miracle. The Bible is the book of books. Its message will cleanse our hearts and transform our lives, and fit us for the work of God. Let us read it on our knees, until its light shall flood our souls and guide us on our heavenly way.

AN UN-NAMED PILGRIM:

On one occasion, some years ago, I stepped off the platform in a mission hall and knelt down beside the most miserable, dishevelled person I have ever set eyes on – a down-and-out tramp. He was comparatively young, yet could not stand up straight. His knees were sticking through his trousers; his feet were bare; his hair was matted over his face. He was utterly hopeless and helpless. I laid my hand on his shoulder and said, 'My friend, I know One who can forgive your sin'. He looked up into my face through his matted hair and said, 'Will you say that again, sir?' and I said it again. He said, 'Come into my home; it is only two or three doors down'. I went into his home; only one room, and it was absolutely bare. There was a mat on one side of the room, and he said, 'That is my bed.' There was a sack lying in the other corner of the room, and he said, 'That is my wife's bed, and that is all we have in the world.' He had done no work for nine years; he had taken a vow that he would not work, and it was the only vow he had ever kept. He was a professional beggar; he told me he could get half-a-crown out of anybody, but it was no use to him, for he went off and drank it away. When he was a boy of fourteen he had run away from home. He had tramped through Scotland; he went out to Africa, joined up during the Boer War. He was wounded and in hospital, and one night he got up and dressed himself in the doctor's clothes, tied a number of sheets together and let himself down out of the window. Months after, he was caught and sentenced to death as a deserter, but on account of his youth he got off. He drifted back to this country and had vowed never to do an honest day's work. He was the most pitiable sight you ever set eyes on. I knelt with him in that little room, and in that place he opened his heart to Christ and the Lord took him out of an horrible pit and from the miry clay, and put a new song into his mouth that people could see.

Six weeks after he was converted, I took him to Spurgeon's Tabernacle. Chapman and Alexander were holding a mission there. Mr Alexander was conducting the singing, and right at the back, I stood with my newly-converted friend. We stood up together and sang, and when we came to the second verse of the song, Alexander said, 'I want you all to stop; there is a man over there in the far distance, and he is singing this song with the light of the glory of heaven in his face. Come up, my brother, and sing us a verse by yourself!' I said to my poor, old, drunken friend, 'Up you go,' and he went up on to the platform and sang a verse by himself and gave his testimony, and Alexander gave him his own song book, and he came back with it under his arm. He never parted with that book.

He went around and found work. God gave him a beautiful home. Every Sunday afternoon his table was laid for six people. He would sit at one end, and his wife at the other. Out into the highways and by-ways he would go until he had four, poor, wretched, miserable fellows, such as he had once been. They would sit down to tea together. There was no vase of flowers in the middle of the table, but in its place was put a family Bible.

After tea there would be a prayer meeting, and the promises of God would be taken for those guests of his. I cannot tell how many hopeless drunkards he led to Christ.

Some few years ago he came to me and said, 'Mr Glegg, I've come to say "Good-bye". My old life has found me out. I'm going into hospital. My ruined body cannot live much longer. I will meet you up yonder.' He went into hospital, and lived there for three weeks. They told me that the men in the beds on each side of him were led to Christ. The nurses spoke of him with tears in their eyes when they thought of the great things that God had done.

*

On Sir Christopher Wren's memorial in St. Paul's Cathedral there are these words: 'If you seek a monument, look around you.' If you seek a monument to the power of the Gospel, look around you at the changed lives of God's people. That is the outward evidence of the value of the message we preach. The ultimate evidence of the all-sufficiency of Christ is seen in the changed, transformed lives of His people. And that is what the world is waiting to see. I believe there are very many hungry people today, ready for the message of the Gospel if they could only see the power of it in your life and mine.

*

Some years ago, I was walking down one of the most beautiful glens in the Highlands of Scotland, arm-in-arm with my friend, the late Dr Stuart Holden. As we came down the hillside together he said to me: 'Do you see that white house down by the edge of the lake among the trees? I will tell you a story about that house. Many well-known people have lunched there; it was a rendezvous for many a shooting and fishing party.

'Years ago, when some celebrated people were there for refreshments, which were being handed round to the company, someone stepped back suddenly and jolted the tray so that the coffee was spilled, and a great ugly mark was made on the white wall. There it was, an unsightly stain. But there was one man in the company, Landseer, perhaps the greatest painter of animal life that this country has known, and he took out a crayon from his pocket, stepped across to the wall and round that ugly stain he began to draw until he had transformed it into a beautiful picture of a Highland stag with its great antlers outstretched.'

My friend said to me: 'You can see that picture today, it has been carefully preserved down the years, and people come from miles to see it.'

The ugly dark blot, the stain, transformed into a thing of beauty, by the touch of a master artist! Is your life just a bit ugly? Are there any stains there? I know of only one remedy. Welcome the Saviour into your life and let Him transform you. He can bring harmony and beauty into your soul. He can turn darkness into light; ugliness into beauty; defeat into victory. He is the Master Spirit, the Great Physician, and His touch has still its ancient power.

*

That famous old Welsh preacher, Christmas Evans, describes in very vivid and picturesque language the home-coming of Legion after the Saviour had set him free. He pictures the wife and children in the house; suddenly the mother cries, 'Children, run for safety, for I see father coming across the fields.' And yet father does not look the same, what has happened to him? Nevertheless, the door must be barred and bolted. Then a strange thing follows; as the terror-stricken wife listens, there comes a gentle knock on the door and she hears her own name – 'Mary, Mary, let me in.' She had not heard that voice since the days when the children first came. Again she listens, 'Mary, let me in, I have seen Jesus'. And in a flash she has unbarred the door and she is in the arms of her husband!

Chapter 8

BIBLE CHARACTERS

'Men of God in days of old were famous for their faith.'
HEBREWS 11 *v* 2

MARTHA and MARY

John ch. 11 tells us a fascinating story of these two sisters. Their brother Lazarus was sick and their thoughts very naturally turned to Jesus, so they decided to send a messenger to Him letting Him know that their brother was ill. What a pity! Why did they not go themselves, of if they could not both be spared one of them might have gone. I am sure Jesus would have come at once. The nobleman came himself to Jesus and his son was healed. The centurian sought out the Master and his servant was healed. Nothing less than a personal visit will do.

In the end it meant an interview with Jesus by both Martha and Mary, but by then Lazarus was dead.

When Jesus drew near to the sorrowing home it must have been Martha who said to Mary 'You go and meet the Master; you know Him so well and He loves you so much' – 'and Mary sat still'. Not a move, so petulant Martha marched out of the room. And when she met Jesus she upbraided Him 'If Thou hadst been here my brother had not died'. In effect she said 'Master, it's your fault'.

How tenderly Jesus spoke to her (John 11. 23-27). What precious words they are, and they brought from Martha her amazing response 'Yea Lord, I believe that

Thou art the Christ, the Son of God' (v.27), and from that moment Martha was changed.

When she returned to Mary, Martha said 'The Master is come and calleth for thee' and in a moment Mary could see that something had happened to Martha. She had never seen her with such a glowing face or heard such a gentle voice, and immediately she 'rose quickly and came to Jesus'. When they met, Mary said the same eleven words that Martha had used, but Mary said them on her knees and in such a tender tone – as if to say 'we so missed You, but You are here now'. There is all the difference in the way we say a thing. What a difference it would make if we could all remember this, in our associations with one another.

One more word before we leave the two sisters. We read 'Jesus wept'. I wonder why? Not because all the others were weeping. There was in front of Jesus, the tomb, and in it lay the body of Lazarus, and as Jesus looked, His thoughts travelled forward to the day when His body would be laid in a tomb, and at that moment His eye caught Mary's eye and He knew she was thinking the same thing, for she alone knew the meaning of the Cross. 'She hath done this against the day of burial' and Jesus was so touched that He wept.

Note the first verse of the next chapter (ch. 12). Thirteen guests in to supper! and 'Martha served'. I can hear Martha saying 'I will see to the meal Mary, you sit at the Master's feet, I can easily manage on my own. The washing up afterwards? Leave that to me also.'

If you think I have no Scriptural authority for all that I have said, I am sure you will forgive me. I wanted to put in a good word for Martha.

THE DISCIPLES:

Our Lord gathered round Him, while on earth, a band of simple, ordinary men and sent them forth as His disciples.

Look at some of them for a moment. There is Peter; impetuous, brave at one moment and a coward at the next. Then, there is John; he was the Son of Thunder, and by no means the meek and mild person he is sometimes pictured as being. John was with Peter when they asked the Lord to send fire down from Heaven to consume an unfriendly Samaritan village. We can quite imagine that Peter and John would not always get on too well together! Then, there was Thomas the materialist, who wanted to see before he would believe. And there was Matthew, the inevitable business man. These business men always turn up. I must not say anything against them as I am one myself, not to mention our chairman, but some of them can be difficult at times!

It was with this material that our Lord had to face the task of turning the world upside down. But ere our Lord departed, He left His disciples this promise, 'If I go away, I will send you another Comforter,' and this promise He fulfilled at Pentecost when the great transformation came. Peter, the coward, became bold and courageous, declaring the death and resurrection of Christ before all men. John and he began to love one another, and together went down to the Gate Beautiful. Matthew used his business ability and, instead of writing out receipts at the Customs House he gave us the first Gospel.

THE GIRL OF 12 IN LUKE 8:

Our Lord Jesus Christ was delayed in the course of one of His journeys; and He came to a home where there lay a little girl of twelve who had been very ill, and had died. There she lay upon the bed; her face was pale; her hands were limp and helpless by her side. And as the Eastern custom was they had brought in a great many people, some doubtless professional mourners, to weep and to wail. And when our Lord came in to that home what did He do? Oh, says someone, I imagine He went straight to the bedside of the little girl, for it was she He had come to bless. No, He did not. He looked around Him, and He said, in effect, 'God can do nothing here. Look at all this unreality; all this moaning and wailing. Let us get the room clear of all that is unreal. And so they turned the people out. And when the doors were shut, Jesus said, 'Mother you will stay, won't you? Father, we shall need you. Peter, James and John, you have been with Me before; you will stay. Now, let us be quiet; and get down to realities!' And the Lord Jesus went to the bedside of the little girl, and stretching out His hand He said, in effect, 'Now, my dear, open your eyes. That's right. Sit up in bed; now you are all right; don't be frightened; it's only Me; now you are feeling better aren't you my dear? Father, will you give her something to eat?' And God had done a big thing. Life had been given. My friend, God wants to do a big thing for you. He wants to give you Christ, and in Christ you will find life, eternal life; you will find in Him love and liberty and all that you need. Every blessing God has for man is in and through Jesus Christ.

THE BOY IN JOHN 6:

How glad we are that Scripture does not overlook the boy who was willing to hand over his lunch. The other Gospels do not mention the boy, but St. John tells us there was a lad in the crowd. Of course there was! Have you ever seen a street accident or a house on fire where a crowd has gathered? I'll guarantee that there will be a lad there who somehow or other has pushed his way into the front row. But this is an unknown boy, for we are not given his name, but we gather from his lunch that he came from a humble home for the fishes were small and the loaves were of barley; the rough, coarse loaf that was given to the Roman prisoners. I suppose the boy's father had been out fishing that morning – I beg your pardon, the father had been out *catching* fish, which is quite a different thing! And having caught some nice ones, he was about to throw the two small ones back when he suddenly thought of the boy at home, and decided to keep them for the lad. So mother baked the barley loaves and the boy was packed off with his lunch in his pocket.

It is wonderful how God has used, down the years, boys who have come from humble homes. We think of such names as Bunyan, Carey, Livingstone, Booth and a countless multitude whom God has raised up from the poor homes of our land to do mighty things in His Name.

The boy, of course, might have thrown his lunch away. He might have said, 'I am not hungry and I am tired of carrying this parcel around with me.' There are plenty of people who are throwing away the opportunities God has given them; they are living careless, selfish lives, drifting with the crowd and getting nowhere, and they will never feed a multitude.

The boy might have said, 'I'll eat my own lunch, after all it is mine, and I see no reason why I should not sit down and enjoy it by myself.' There are people who speak like that today. They say, 'I must develop my own life, follow my own instincts and fill a place in the world of my own choice.' Yes, but you will never feed a multitude that way.

And once more, the boy might have divided his lunch among the few. He might have spotted a friend in the crowd and given him a fish or perhaps share a loaf with one of his young school friends. There are many people today who make a religion out of 'doing good'. They glory in the fact that they pay their way, that they are good neighbours, that they help many good causes, but remember, you will never feed a multitude that way.

The all-inclusive secret is to give your all to Jesus Christ, 'And Jesus took the loaves'. This is the very heart of the story; this is the key to the miracle.

PAUL:

The Apostle was kept busy from morning till evening; he put in a full day's work – no eight hours a day for Paul! He could say: 'I laboured more abundantly than they all.'

The chief men of the Jews in Rome came to his lodging: I wonder why? Was it because it was such a wonderful place? Such a magnificent establishment? So beautifully furnished, and the very last word in fashion? Did they say to one another, 'It is worth your while to go and see Paul's new lodgings?' The word used in the Greek means a very humble apartment, and not even in the best part of the city. It was in this modest abode that Paul, although a gentleman to his finger tips, and a highly cultured man, spent his days, and the people flocked to see him. They went because they were hungry for spiritual food; they came 'in great number' because they wanted the teaching and counsel that Paul could give them.

Then, I believe, there was the attractive power of Paul's personality. The very fragrance of his life drew people to him, and they came to ask him for the secret.

Paul, your life is like a fairy tale; you went out to be shipwrecked, to be beaten; you went out to be despised of friends and forsaken; you went out for God and anywhere and everywhere. Paul, where did you get your faith from? Paul says, I got it by venturing out for God, and as I went out for Him, He went with me, and my faith grew and my doubts went.

The Apostle Paul said: 'I bear branded on my body the marks of the Lord Jesus.' There he was, a gentleman to his finger tips, highly educated, sensitive, a wonderful mind, a tender spirit. And he goes through this world to be beaten, and persecuted for Christ's sake. He tells us: 'Five times received I forty stripes save one.' It was a punishment rarely inflicted to the full. Most criminals. fell unconscious under the blows before the thirty-ninth. Many a man never lived through it. And yet five times the apostle bared his back to receive the full penalty. He was

shipwrecked; he was buffeted on every hand. Poor, despised man, bent and broken, perhaps an insignificant-
looking man; but there he was bearing in his body the
marks of the Lord Jesus.

PAUL & SILAS:

I would like to have heard Paul and Silas singing: it must
have been a wonderful duet. I think Paul would take the
tenor part – he would reach the top notes all right and
not get wrecked on the high C's as some of us do!

DAVID:

When David faced Goliath we are told that he went down
to the brook, and he chose five smooth pebbles. I always
used to wonder why he took five stones. Did he think he
was going to miss Goliath the first four times, and that he
had better have a fifth stone? No, David was possessed
of a magnificent aim with a sling; I doubt if he ever
missed anything. In the East today I am told that a
shepherd will put his rod, or staff in the ground, and he
will walk back thirty or forty paces, and he will fling a
stone, and hit that rod, or staff, every time. David only
needed one stone for Goliath; he could hit his mark
with a certainty. Why then, did he take five stones?

Well, if you read further on in the Scriptures you will
discover that Goliath had four sons. So David really
needed those five stones. What is the good of killing a
giant if you leave four of his sons roaming about; they
will soon grow up and be as tall and strong as their father!
We have got to slay every foe; there is no excuse for
failing. In Christ we have God's perfect solution, and
when we have failed we have only ourselves to blame.

MATTHEW:

Matthew must have been a clever man, for it was necessary for him to speak several languages before he could take that position. I suppose it is right to infer that he must have been a cunning man, and a cruel boastful man also. The Romans in appointing a tax collector, chose a district, auctioned it, and the highest bidder got the appointment. All he was concerned to do was to pay over to the Roman authorities the amount of revenue required, and the balance went into his own pocket. Matthew thought to himself, 'That's the job for me! I can make good at that business.'

I think Matthew was a married man. Have you noticed how that, in his account of the feeding of the 5,000 men, he alone adds the significant touch – 'besides women and children'. (Matth. 14.21.) Matthew throws up his job at the call of Christ. And what can Matthew do? He has pen in his hand, and he yields it to the Master, and with that pen gives us the first Gospel. Once again, it is the same principle – first surrender, then service.

PETER:

Peter was a young man though married, living with his mother-in-law he must have been very young! – and his weakness is transformed into strength.

THOMAS:

There is an old legend about Thomas, that after he had seen the risen Lord and had said, 'My Lord and my God!' he fell into doubt once again.

He went to see Peter, James and John. All were busy and could not help him. He found his way to Dorcas, and

Dorcas was knitting and stitching away when Thomas came in and said, 'I am full of doubt again, Dorcas, do help me.' Dorcas said, 'Look here, Thomas, go out and do something, go and tell somebody that Christ died for their sins and rose again according to the Scriptures.' And Thomas went out and said to the first man he met, 'Do you know that Christ lives? He died for our sins, but He rose again.' And there Thomas and that stranger went on their knees together and both rose up triumphant in the faith.

Lead someone else to the Saviour; help somebody else. See the power of this message at work in other hearts. That is the way to get rid of your own doubts.

ZACCHAEUS:

I look on Zacchaeus as a middle-aged man, at the zenith of his career. The only thing against my theory is that he climbed a tree! But who would not climb a tree to see the Saviour? Zacchaeus had, no doubt, heard of this great Teacher who was to pass by, and he decided he must see this Man. His first difficulty was that he was too low down. That physical limitation illustrates a spiritual difficulty. Some people, today, think that they have fallen too low for Christ to reach them; but, thank God no one is outside the reach of His love.

So Zacchaeus climbed a tree, and his next difficulty was that he was too high up, and Christ had to say to him, 'Come down'. It is all too common to find people who are too high up in their own esteem, and the trouble is that they are not ready to come down. Christ calls to the man, 'Zacchaeus, make haste and come down; for today I must abide at thy house' (Luke 19.5.); and this middle-aged man gives his immediate response, and owns his allegiance to Christ. He 'believes on the name of His Son Jesus Christ.' and the outcome? 'The half of my goods I give to the poor.'

Chapter 9

THINGS CONCERNING HIMSELF

'Jesus interpreted to them in all the Scriptures the things concerning Himself.'

LUKE 24 *v* 27 (RSV)

In that wonderful day you will say, 'Thank the Lord! praise His name! Tell the world about His wondrous love. How mighty He is!' Sing to the Lord, for He has done wonderful things. Make known His praise around the world.

ISAIAH 12 *vs* 4/5

O Patient, spotless one,
Our hearts in meekness train
To bear Thy yoke, and learn from Thee,
That we may rest obtain.

Jesus! Thou art enough
The mind and heart to fill;
Thy patient life-to calm the soul;
Thy love-its fear dispel.

O fix our earnest gaze
So wholly, Lord, on Thee,
That, with Thy beauty occupied,
We elsewhere none may see.

C. A. Bernstein (1672-1699)

I have seen the face of Jesus
Tell me not of aught beside,
I have heard the voice of Jesus
All my soul is satisfied.

THINGS CONCERNING HIMSELF:

Our Lord was wonderful *in the way He fulfilled prophecy.*
A friend of mine wrote out in full 120 prophecies in the
Old Testament concerning our Lord's first coming, and
in a parallel column he wrote the fulfilment of those
prophecies as recorded in the New Testament showing
that when, in God's appointed time, Jesus came, He
fulfilled every prophecy concerning His birth, His life,
and His death – wonderful!

And although there is a gap of at least 400 years
between the Old and New Testaments of our Bible, the
Son of God fulfilled to the letter all that was foretold
concerning His first coming.

He was wonderful in His birth. Such a life demands a
wonderful beginning. Oh! If man had planned it, if man
had written the story and staged the whole thing, how
different it would have been. Man would have chosen a
palace; but God chose a barn. Man would have clothed
the little Babe in silken garments; but God chose that
He should be wrapped in swaddling clothes. Man
would have filled the place with perfume and odours
sweet and beautiful but God chose that the little Babe
should be born amidst the odours of a stable.

Jesus was wonderful also *in His Life.* What a life it is!
Have you been reading the life of the Saviour lately,
reading right through it to catch something of the wonder
and the glory of it? I hope you have not lost the power
to wonder. The young people of the present day get so
blasé. Nothing seems to please them; they can't wonder
at anything. They live in such an age of scientific discovery, *that nothing startles them.* Read the life of Christ,
and see if the Holy Spirit does not startle you with the
very wonder and the beauty of all He said and did. He
could say to the winds and the waves, 'Be still!' They are
strong words. It is just as if He turned to the winds and
waves, and said, 'Shut up!' But the same voice that rang
out a rebuke to the storm could say, 'Suffer the little

children to come unto Me, and forbid them not, for of such is the Kingdom of Heaven.'

He was wonderful in His life. He wrote no book, and yet all the presses down the ages have ground out literature and books about Him that have filled our libraries. He founded no college, and yet He has baffled all the world's learning and scholarship.

Then He was *wonderful in His death*. He chose the very time when He should die. He is the only One ever born into this world whose great purpose, whose great climax in life was to be His death, and then a wondrous resurrection.

*

Who was *responsible* for Christ's death? What was the cause? The enmity of the Jews? The weakness of Pilate? The cry of the angry mob? No, we must look beyond the Roman spear, and the howling mob. Peter was right when he wrote: 'Who being delivered by the determinate counsel and foreknowledge of God, ye have taken, and by wicked hands have crucified and slain.' Yes, God was responsible. 'It pleased the Lord to bruise Him.' 'He hath put Him to grief.' Christ was not a martyr slain by an angry crowd. The life and the death of Christ were determined by God in every detail. There have been many martyrs, and they have died rejoicing. Listen to one as he sings, 'I shall breakfast below on fiery tribulation, but before night I will sup with Christ.' Here is another, 'I value these chains as if they had been gold.' And yet another, 'O Christ, how sweet to die!'

But turn to the Cross. At the Cross there is no song: there is no exultation. There in the Garden our Lord prays, 'If it is possible let this cup pass from Me.' And on the Cross He cries, 'My God, My God, why hast Thou forsaken Me?' The heavens are darkened. The presence of God has been with every dying saint: but the presence of

God was denied Christ. It was not a martyr dying. It was God giving His only begotten Son.

*

Sometimes in describing the Cross, preachers will give you the idea that by reason of exhaustion and exposure to the heat of the midday sun, and by all that He had gone through, by the cruel nails in His hands and feet, with the consequent loss of blood and weakness, Jesus grows weaker and weaker until His life ebbs away into unconsciousness, and soon His Spirit has gone. But that is not how Christ died. 'He cried with a *loud voice*, It is finished! And He gave up the ghost.' He dismissed His Spirit by an act of His own will. Why, if a man is dying of exhaustion, slipping gradually into unconsciousness, you bend down your head to catch his last whisper. But all four Gospels emphasise this fact that Jesus on the Cross cried out with a loud, ringing voice, 'It is finished!' With a voice that reached out over Jerusalem, with a voice that sounded across the horizon. It was the cry of a Man in the vigour of His manhood. And by an act of His own will He dismissed His spirit. It was a voluntary sacrifice.

Chapter 10

PARTNERS IN THE GOSPEL

'They beckoned to their partners in the other boat to come and help them.'

LUKE 5 *v* 7 (RSV)

'Since we have such a huge crowd of men of faith watching us from the grandstands, let us strip off anything that slows us down or holds us back, and especially those sins that wrap themselves so tightly around our feet and trip us up; and let us run with patience the particular race that God has set before us.'

HEBREWS 12 *v* 1

'Remember your leaders who have taught you the word of God. Think of all the good that has come from their lives, and try to trust the Lord as they do.'

HEBREWS 13 *v* 7

GENERAL WILLIAM BOOTH:

When the founder of the Salvation Army preached in Brixton Theatre he came to stay for the weekend at my father's house in Clapham Park. I remember his secretary coming prior to the General's visit to make the necessary arrangements. The general had our best spare room, while the secretary was given a room one floor above. I was intrigued to see the secretary fixing a bell-push by the side of the bed to be occupied by the General, and carrying a wire up the stairs to his own room where a battery and bell were connected up. On asking what all this was for the secretary replied, 'The General might be ill in the night and require me; he might even die in the night and I must be by his side to take down his last words.' Happily there were no signs of the General dying; he kept us very much alive over the weekend. He was no trouble to entertain for *he* entertained *us*; and my mother had no worries concerning his welfare for his secretary cooked all his meals in the kitchen and served them up at the table along with what our own cook had provided for the family. I will never forget the General's face or his sermon in the Brixton Theatre. He gripped you by his dominating personality. His piercing eyes seemed to look right through you, and his long white beard made you think of the rugged prophets of old. Has anybody ever lived who has so justly been described as the greatest organiser in the world, one who built up the great Salvation Army which has reached across the world, and yet one who was entirely dominated by a consuming passion for the souls of men. The General preached that night in the Theatre on The Flood and his very appearance almost made one think that Noah himself had returned to warn us of judgement to come. I can see him now describing the breaking of the storm and the men beating on the door of the ark and in their anguish crying out, 'My God! it's shut.' After supper on the Sunday evening we gathered round the fire and the General told us stories. At 11 o'clock his secretary knocked at the door and reminded the General of the time. This was repeated at 11.30 and again at midnight, when my father intervened and thought the General ought to retire. My brother and I were fascinated by these vivid stories. My father found the General was very interested in the problems of unemployment and of social conditions, and when they met again some years later the General picked up the conversation exactly where it had left off. At that time the General was being attacked for hoarding up money for himself and getting rich. In my enthusiasm to defend him I asked him if this were true. His reply was interesting.

'I don't own a penny,' he said, 'when I die I shall have nothing to leave. It's a long time since I have had a coin in my pocket. If I need a haircut someone in the Army will see to it for me, if I want a new hat the Army will provide it. What do I want any money for?'

General Booth once put his hand on my shoulder and said: 'Young man, I never had the chance in life that you have had; I never had the upbringing or the education that you have had.' What then was the secret of his success? Some of you will remember how fond he was of saying: 'There came a day in my life when I said to God, Lord, Thou shalt have all there is of William Booth! And from that moment God blessed me.'

DR G. CAMPBELL MORGAN:

Campbell Morgan was one of the men who influenced me most. He was at his height in Westminster Chapel when I was eager for Bible truth. His Friday evening Bible School attracted people of all ages and of many different denominations, and it was there that he laid the foundation of Biblical truth for me, on which foundation I have tried to build for fifty years or more. Campbell Morgan was a born preacher. There were two places where he was really happy – in his study and in his pulpit. I have always thought he would have made a great actor; his voice and his gestures were perfect and he spoke with such authority and assurance. He was a preacher and he loved his vocation. He left personal work largely to others; he preferred addressing a thousand people rather than one. The last time I heard him preach he asked me kindly to sit with him in the pulpit at Westminster and I was interested to see his sermon notes. He had three separate sheets laid out on the pulpit Bible. On the first was typed his opening sentences. On the middle sheet there were four headings only, and on the third sheet there was a closely typed manuscript of the finish of his sermon. I learned much from this; how valuable it is for the sermon to start well; but, once in your stride, don't be tied to your notes; but be careful you know just how you are going to finish. What a lot of sermons fade out weakly without getting anywhere. Fortunately many of Campbell Morgan's sermons are in print but they inevitably miss the light and shade of his voice, his perfect elocution and the dramatic way in which he drove home his message.

*

There is a beautiful story in the biography of *Dr G. Campbell Morgan*. He has four sons, and they are all preachers. His youngest son, Howard, took his father's place on the other side of the Atlantic when Dr Morgan came to London, and Howard is considered to be a great preacher. Someone once came into the drawing-room when all the family were there. They thought they would see what Howard was made of, and they asked him this question, 'Howard, who is the greatest preacher in your family?' Howard had a great admiration for his father, and he looked straight across at him and then, without a moment's hesitation, he answered, 'Mother'.

Howard Morgan was right! Mothers very often are the best preachers; some of them who have never stood on platforms or in pulpits are preaching the greatest sermons! You may carry the glory of the Lord with you, and shed it abroad as much by the beauty of your life as by the eloquence of your lips.

MARTIN LUTHER:

Martin Luther, how did you strengthen your faith? You broke the fetters of priesthood and ignorance; you became a mighty man of God. Yes, because Martin Luther ventured out for God, he saw the light and he stepped

into it. He heard the call and he responded; he obeyed
and his faith grew until he became triumphant.

DR ALEXANDER WHYTE:

I was once holiday-making in the pretty village of Ew-
hurst in Surrey. There was no Free Church in the village
but a barn was made use of, a few chairs were brought in
and a local capenter had knocked up a little platform,
and with a small reading desk, the chapel was complete.
The services were in charge of a gardener who, without
much education, had a real love for the Lord, and who
knew his Bible, He reminded me of the old Puritan who
said, 'I am only an old rag, Lord, but I am soaked in Thy
Word, now take me out and squeeze me that somebody
else may get the benefit.'

I found my way one Sunday morning into this barn
with ten or a dozen friends; there may have been two or
three local people besides. That morning there walked
on to the platform an elderly gentleman with long white
hair. He had a personality that gripped you at once and I
knew we were in for a treat (if such a phrase may be
allowed). He opened the Bible at Psalm 103 and, after
these many years, I can still remember his words; he was
at home among the Puritans and Bunyan. He illustrated
the waywardness of human nature by the game of bowls
where the wood had a bias that took it off the straight.
Not until the service was over did I discover that we had
been sitting at the feet of Dr Alexander Whyte of St.
George's, Edinburgh, who must surely be numbered
among the mightiest preachers in living memory.

W. P. NICHOLSON:

God undoubtedly did a tremendous work through him
in Northern Ireland. Thousands of souls were brought to

the Lord by 'W.P.' and many are in the ministry today.
He came over to London to St. Paul's, Portman Square,
for Dr Stuart Holden, but apart from this, I think I am
the only one who had been venturesome enough to invite
him to conduct a mission in London. He came to us in
1928 for a special effort at Down Lodge Hall, London
S.W. He shocked a great many of my people with his
rough tongue, but it was no use trying to change him.
My wife and I did our best, with, I'm afraid, no success,
but still the people came and many were converted. Dr
Graham Scroggie once said to me, 'He is filled with
vulgarity and with the Holy Spirit, and how a man can be
filled with both at the same time I don't know.' Neither
do I.

The secret of his power was no doubt in his prayer life.
He stayed at our home for ten days during the campaign
and he was up in the morning at six o'clock, but he never
appeared until twelve noon, he spent the hours wrestling
with God in prayer. My wife would take up his breakfast
and leave it outside his bedroom door, but it was rarely
taken in. By his own special request he was not disturbed
by phone or visitor, however urgent. He conducted a
campaign for the students at Cambridge at the request of
the Christian Union, and my wife and I went up to help.
We met Willie Nicholson in his room for prayer and afterwards my wife, walking across to his bed, said, 'What have
you been up to, your sheets are torn into shreds?' 'Ah,'
said Willie, 'I must tell them at the office about that.'
What had happened was that he, unconsciously, ago-
nizing in prayer, had ripped the sheets into strips with
his strong hands and arms. Yes, prayer was surely the
secret of his power.

BISHOP TAYLOR SMITH:

The *Bishop* and I were often doubled together as speakers
at Conventions. I used to like being with him except

that he never knew when to stop! He had little idea of time; he had a very placid temperament and was never in a hurry, so my address had to be like a concertina, which I could pull out or push in according to the time available.

The Bishop's greatest work was done in talking to people individually; at this he was a master hand. God gave him the gift and he did not neglect to use it. I have been with him on walks and in railway trains and I have often marvelled how smoothly he could lead the conversation into spiritual channels. I actually received a letter from him two weeks after his decease! He died on board ship and of course the letter could not be posted until the boat arrived in harbour.

I remember hearing (from one who was present) of a meeting in New York where Bishop Taylor Smith was announced to speak. He had caught a cold on the boat crossing over to America and arrived at the meeting with practically no voice. My friend told me that only those in the very front seats could hear the Bishop, the rest of the vast auditorium never heard a word; and yet the Bishop held his audience spell-bound for 40 minutes! At the close of the service a man from the top gallery came forward to my friend and told him that the service had marked the turning point in his life. He said: 'I could not hear a word the Bishop said, not even a sound reached me, but I looked, and there on the platform stood a man of God, his lips moving and occasionally an upraised hand, and God spoke to my soul, and in the quietness I slipped down on to my knees and surrendered my life to Christ.'

DR STUART HOLDEN:

My friend, the late Dr Stuart Holden, was sitting one day in the lounge at his club, and a number of people round him were discussing golf. Presently one of them turned and said, 'By the way, Holden, what is your handicap?' and without a moment's pause Dr Holden replied, '*Myself!*' How true that is – Self – the Capital 'I' is the universal problem, the handicap of us all.

The Apostle Paul recognised this when he said, 'O wretched man that I am, who shall deliver me from the body of this death?' Or, as it is in another translation: 'Who shall deliver me from this dead body?'

It was a sad loss when Dr Holden left us at the comparatively early age of fifty-nine. He might have lived longer but I could not persuade him to take up golf! I am certain preachers need exercises – something that will take their minds off their work. C. H. Spurgeon died before he was sixty, and it is said that he worked twelve to sixteen hours a day. It is true that Holden was fond of fishing and caught many a salmon, but that was during his summer holiday in Scotland. When his homecall came I wrote of him: 'His messages were amongst the choicest and most beautiful ever delivered at Keswick; in eloquence he was a giant and yet he was the most approachable of men. What a unique command of English language he had. He was the most charming and interesting companion I ever met, and yet he was a great listener, so sympathetic and gentle. Surely his gifts were unique, and it is no wonder that hundreds flocked to him with their problems and sorrows; and from the highest to the lowest he was ever ready to help. He was generous with his time and money almost to a fault, and he literally wore himself out in his service for others.'

GIPSY SMITH

When my sister Helen was married she lived next door to Gipsy Smith in Cambridge, and from then on we were friends. In his early days he was with the Salvation Army and I can remember his telling me how he severed his connection. He had conducted a great campaign in the

Midlands and at the close he was presented with a gold watch suitably engraved. On returning to London he showed the watch with some justifiable pride to the General. William Booth looked at the watch with interest and appreciation and then slipped the watch into a drawer in his desk and closed the drawer. 'But I want my watch back,' said the Gipsy, quite naturally. The General took out the watch, placed it in the palm of his left hand and stretched out also his right hand.

'You must make your choice,' said the General; 'if you take the watch then clasp my right hand and bid farewell to the Army.' The Gipsy left the S.A. headquarters with his watch – but no longer a Salvationist. The General laid down rules for the working of the Salvation Army and could not make exceptions; no private gifts were allowed.

I loved to hear Gipsy Smith preach. He could seemingly do what he liked with an audience. One moment the listening crowd would be rocking with laughter, the next moment they would be in tears.

TORREY AND ALEXANDER

I heard Torrey and Alexander in the Royal Albert Hall in 1905, and later at Brixton where they moved over to a temporary building. Charles Alexander was the greatest song-leader of my generation and perhaps the greatest ever in evangelical work. He trained a large choir at the Albert Hall (one member of the choir become my wife five years later), but before long the whole audience was his choir for they responded so perfectly to his beat. Indeed before long all London seemed to be singing the Glory Song; the barrel organs, so common in those days, ground out the tune at the street corners, the messenger boy whistled it, tunefully or otherwise, as he went on his way, and time and again Alexander had to sing it in response to repeated requests. It was a great thrill for me to see men and women seeking Christ under the very clear but somewhat stern preaching of the Gospel by Dr Torrey.

Later on while Chapman and Alexander toured the world together I always tried to be present when they came to Britain. I can remember one meeting in Edinburgh, for old people; no one under sixty-five was allowed. It was held in the afternoon and I happened to be in Scotland on business. I can remember Alexander appealing the night before for people to lend their carriages and carts to bring in the folk. What a sight it was to see them arriving; farmers had lent their carts and wagons, every kind of vehicle was commissioned to bring in the aged. One old man was brought in a wheel-barrow; he was duly tipped out by his friend who trundled off with his barrow to fetch someone else.

During the meeting Alexander asked those over seventy to rise to their feet and hundreds responded. Then those over seventy-five were asked to stand, then the over eighties, then the over eighty-five and ninety groups.

There was a hush in the meeting when Alexander asked, 'Is there anyone here ninety-five or over?' A pause followed and then an old man with a long beard rose slowly to his feet, ninety-five years old. A friend of mine, Rev. Edward Last, after the meeting led that dear man to Christ. A soul saved at the eleventh hour, but a life lived and lost to God.

LIONEL FLETCHER

I learned a great deal from Lionel Fletcher and followed his method of drawing in the net, a method which Billy Graham uses with such effect today. Lionel was a great story-teller; his illustrations were unique. He used to say to me, 'Don't hurry the telling of your illustrations; tell them well, build up the background, picture the whole scene and make it live before the eyes of your congregation. I will take,' he said, 'ten valuable minutes if necessary to tell a story.' Many of his vivid stories live in my memory today and, with them, the truths they illustrated.

F. B. MEYER

There are some people whose looks do not attract you towards them, but Dr Meyer was a saint and looked like one; with his quiet manner and his gentle voice, one's life was enriched by being in his presence. Almost the last thing he ever did was to send me a postcard. He was lying ill in Boscombe and with a shaky hand he wrote, 'I have raced you to heaven, I am just off, see you there, Love, F. B. Meyer.' The story was told of him that he asked the Doctor how much longer he had to live. The doctor replied, 'Just a few more hours, say to 4 o'clock.' At this Dr Meyer went to sleep and awoke later in the afternoon. His first question was, 'What is the time, nurse?' 'Six o'clock,' she replied, 'Tut, tut,' said Meyer, 'this will never do, I ought to have gone two hours ago.' I can well believe this story to be true; he was a pilgrim down here, his real home was in Heaven.

It is strange how apparently unimportant remarks come back to one's memory. I remember Dr Meyer saying to me, 'Always travel first class when you are on your way to speak at a meeting; I always do, you have room to spread out your papers and study, and you arrive fresh and prepared for your meeting.' This may largely account for the fact that he could stand up to endless railway journeys, even when he was over eighty years of age.

I can also remember his saying to me, 'Do not be afraid of bringing a little humour into your message; I try to, even if I have to drag in a story, generally about half way through my address. You can't keep your audience tensed up all the time; you must allow them to relax; remember laughter and tears lie closely together.'

F. B. Meyer lived a very full life, he preached here, there and everywhere. He was a minister of three famous churches and he wrote many books. I once asked him how he did it all, and he replied, 'God has been very good to me; I can do quite well on four hours sleep at night. I study up to 2 a.m., then retire to bed until 6 a.m., when I rise and get ready for the day before me.

*

Dr F. B. Meyer often used to say that he did not know the day nor the hour when he first trusted Christ. He could never point to any experience that memory brought back to him. He knew there was a moment when he passed from death unto life: and he used to say, 'When I get to the glory land I will look up the records there, and I will find the day and the hour when my name was written in the Book of Life.'

BROWNLOW NORTH

Away in the City of Aberdeen there once came a great evangelist, whose name was Brownlow North, one of the famous preachers of his time. He was to speak in one of the largest churches of the city, and it was thronged with people who wished to hear him. While sitting in the vestry before the service, a note was handed in to him from an old companion of his unregenerate days. The letter challenged Brownlow North to enter the pulpit. 'I know your past history,' the writer declared; 'I followed you to Paris years ago, and I know your career of sin and vice. I have a record of your life at Liverpool, and I know how you carried on in Manchester, and I challenge you to stand in a Christian pulpit and preach – I dare you to do it.'

Brownlow North went up into the pulpit and commenced the service by reading the letter. He missed out nothing, reading out a long list of vile sins, and then he turned to the congregation and said: 'My friends, it is all true, and a good deal more is true than even my old companion has written. But I want to tell you that there came a day in my life when I heard the Saviour's voice saying, "Brownlow North, go in peace, thy sins are forgiven thee," and if there was mercy for me, there is mercy for all of you here.'

The service did not continue as had been arranged, for men and women were broken down there and then. Many hundreds surrendered to God that night, weeping their way into the kingdom, and a mighty work was started in the old granite city that is spoken of until this day.

CHAPMAN

We must catch a vision of this lost and starving world. I used to love to hear Chapman and Alexander as they went forth conducting missions together. Chapman used to describe how, in his younger days, he once stood on the edge of a cliff and watched a ship wrecked on the rocks. The storm was so great that no help could be given and Chapman watched the great waves wash all the men but one, overboard. The solitary remaining figure clung to the rigging, it was his only hope, but alas, he also was soon dashed into the sea. As Chapman watched, he heard, above the noise of the storm, the last cry of the drowning man as he lifted up his voice and shouted, 'lost – lost – lost!'

To the end of his days Chapman could hear ringing in his mind the despairing cry of that dying man. And there on the top of the cliff he bowed his head and offered his life without reserve to God, pledging himself to go, if need be, to the ends of the earth to seek and save the lost.

Chapter 11

NATURE OUR TEACHER

'Does not nature itself teach you ... ?'
I CORINTHIANS 11 *v* 14

'Consider the lilies of the field, how they grow; they neither toil nor spin.'
MATTHEW 6 *v* 28

O Lord, what a variety You have made! And in wisdom You have made them all! The earth is full of Your riches. There before me lies the mighty ocean, teeming with life of every kind, both great and small. And look! See the ships! And over there, the whale you made to play in the sea. Every one of these depends on You to give them daily food. You supply it and they gather it. You open wide your hand to feed them and they are satisfied with all your bountiful provision.
PSALM 104 *vs* 24/28

WEEDS IN THE GARDEN POND:

I was speaking not long ago to one of the big landscape gardeners in London. He was telling me that he had laid out a garden for a lady, and built her a pond. One of the best ways to line a pond and keep it water-tight, is to puddle it with clay, and he thought that as the District Railway were boring a new tunnel, it would be a great opportunity for him to obtain some real, solid, London clay for his purpose, and he got it for the cost of cartage.

The clay seemed most suitable for the purpose, so he

lined the bottom of the pond with it, and it looked first-class in every respect. One day, when the spring came round, he received a telephone call from the lady, requesting him to come and look at the pond. Great was his surprise to find that it was full of weeds. He told me that growing up in the pond were some weeds which he had never seen before in his life. The lady, very naturally, said to him, 'This is no good,' and, indeed, he had to empty the pond and take out all the clay.

This is what had happened. Away down in the heart of London, forty feet under the streets, in the solid clay, were embedded the seeds of weeds. Given the right environment, the needed light and water, those seeds came to life. Similarly, if we give self a chance it will produce the works of the flesh, and you and I will fall into sin. Let us be quite clear about it. If we have been consecrated Christians for twenty, thirty, or even forty years, and we take our eyes off the Saviour, we give the old fallen nature a chance to have its own way, and it will drag us back into sin.

A GREAT OAK TREE:

I was once looking at a great oak tree. Scientists tell us that that oak tree will probably give out every summer to the atmosphere something like 120 tons of water by simple evaporation from its leaves! What a tremendous output! It is capable of drawing up hundreds of buckets of water every twenty-four hours on a summer's day. How is it done? What draws the water up that tree? Is it capillary attraction? Is it some root pressure? Is it because there is a vacuum there and the atmosphere without presses the water up? None of these things can explain it. It is a mystery. All you can say is this: there is life within, and that life within does the impossible thing.

A young man may be irritable and discontented and

defeated. And in a few days' time he may be sweet and restful and victorious and joyful! What has happened? It is the Spirit of God dwelling in him. It is the life within. We cannot explain it, but that young man has opened his heart to the incoming of the very life of God, and that life has transformed him. There may be a girl who is proud and selfish. But the Lord Jesus meets with her, and she kneels at His feet, and she goes back, humble and gracious and loving, – displaying the very beauty of Christ wherever she goes. How does it happen? Why, the Spirit of God possesses her and fills her, the very life of God coming in, brings about a glorious transformation.

A PALM TREE:

'The righteous shall flourish like a palm tree.' Psalm 92:12. The characteristic of the palm tree is that it grows from the inside. Our distinctive British trees like the elm and the oak grow from the outside. Each year they add a circle of growth so that if you cut an oak or elm horizontally you will see the rings of growth and you can tell the age of the tree by counting the rings. Indeed, you may tell something of the history of the tree: a fat ring indicates that it was a good year for the tree. If the ring of growth is a narrow one it means that the tree has had a lean year. And so the history of the tree is written just as the story of our lives is recorded in Heaven. But not so with the palm tree. It grows from the centre outwards. And the Christian experience is not putting on something from the outside, it is not an outward profession, nor the keeping of certain religious observances. These things, good and wise as they may be, do not in themselves make a Christian. Christianity is a matter of the heart, and the only way to become a Christian is to reckon on what Christ accomplished for us on Calvary's Cross, and to receive Him into our hearts a living Saviour.

AN ELM TREE'S LEAVES:

One year I was wending my way to the early morning prayer meeting at the Keswick Convention when a friend came round the corner and said, 'Good morning, will you tell me how many leaves there are on a full-grown elm tree?' I gave it up. 'But you have not stopped to think,' he said. 'No,' I said, 'I have got very little brain, and I have to take care of it in the early morning!' 'Well,' he said, 'I will tell you.' 'All right, I will take your word for it; I am not going to spend my summer holiday counting them.' 'Well,' he said, 'there are a million leaves on a full grown elm tree.' And I waited to hear what he was going to say next: I thought he would follow it up with something good – 'A million leaves, and they are *all different.*' How true that is; God never made two leaves alike. He always creates originals. You are unique, and so am I. There's nobody else in the whole world like me (and some of you may say, 'That's a jolly good thing'; but it's true). We are all different. We have a witness to give this world and if we are not giving it, the world is the poorer, and the Church is the poorer. Are you ready for this call? The same men; the same equipment; the same place? Will you go back there now to give your simple quiet witness for God?

A FROG:

I am told that if a frog is placed in a bowl of water, and the water heated very gradually, so gradually indeed, that the frog is unconscious of any increase of temperature from one moment to another, the frog can be actually boiled alive without moving or showing any sign of discomfort. The devil practises the art of slow approach to perfection. How methodically he sets to work. How insidiously he worms his way in until the whole world is in an uproar.

FOXGLOVE SEEDS:

When I built my house twenty and more years ago, I chose a spot that was beautifully wooded on the top of Kingston Hill. I said to my wife: 'We shall think we are out in the country with all these trees around us.' My wife replied, 'But where are the foxgloves?' For we in Surrey do not consider we are really out in the country until we see the foxgloves growing wild in the woods and lanes. I at once promised to scatter the seed and give her all the foxgloves she desired. But alas, I forgot my promise. Soon the builders were digging out the foundations for the house and coming upon some good soil for the garden. This I had spread over the beds and under the trees and in due course the house was built and we had taken up residence. Then came the spring with the primroses first and then the bluebells and then – to my astonishment – there came up everywhere, foxgloves! There were none in the neighbouring gardens or woodlands; I had got them all! But where did they come from? It was a long time before I solved the problem. When the builders dug out the foundations and scattered the soil, it was doubtless full of the seeds of foxgloves. How long had they lain buried? A hundred years, a thousand years? I do not know, but when the seed was brought up under the influence of the sun and the rain from above, the seed germinated and the blossom came.

There are many people moving among us today into whose heart the seed has fallen. Perhaps it was sown by a faithful Sunday School teacher, perhaps it was the memory of that childlike prayer that was learnt from mother's lips. But the seed has lain dormant. Could God use your testimony to be as the sun and rain from Heaven to some needy soul? It may be a letter that you write, or booklet that you pass on, or a kindly word spoken in Christ's name and behold the seed is springing into life.

Chapter 12

PERSONAL REMINISCENCES

FISHING:

I remember fishing once in Scotland, in the river Dee.
I had just bought a brand new rod, and a complete fishing
outfit, and I stood on the banks of the Dee, with all my
wonderful tackle, ready to catch a fine haul of fish. My
twin sisters were also there. They were then about seven
years of age; and they wanted to fish. I told them they
were disturbing the sport, but I could not satisfy them
until I had cut a stick off a tree, and tied on it a piece of
string, with a bent pin at the end, on to which I attached
a worm. I sent them down the stream to fish for themselves, so that they might leave me undisturbed while I
went on angling with my perfect tackle.

I caught nothing, but hearing a shout from the direction of my sisters, I looked and saw a wonderful trout.
I do not exaggerate when I say it was a finer fish than any
I caught during the whole of that summer. There it was
on the grass bank, and as I ran down the bank of the
river, I asked, 'What has happened?' 'Oh,' said one of the
girls, 'I have caught this!'

There is plenty of organization in the Church today.
The equipment is all right. We are all very polished, we
have everything just so, but we are not catching fish!
And this poor old world is perishing! It is not wonderful
tackle the Lord wants. He wants simple people to live in
vital touch with Him; and I want to ask in my Lord's
name – Will you be one of them? Will you come into
living, vital touch with Him, and then go out to pass on

the blessing – to overflow to others, to be a witness for your Lord?

A WATER BUTT:

Some years ago, when my twin boys were very young, one Saturday afternoon I was looking at a little conservatory which we had in the garden. There was no gutter along the top, and I thought that it would be a nice Saturday afternoon's task for me to put a gutter there, then a down-pipe to a water butt, so that we might have it full of rain water for the benefit of the garden. I rolled up my sleeves and got to work, and finished the job to the satisfaction of the family. Then we went to bed, and that night down came the rain. As I lay awake listening to the downpour, I pictured in my mind the water rising in the butt. Before breakfast, I went down with the family to see the splendid result, but when we looked inside the water butt, it was empty!

Some kind friend had come along, after we had gone in, and said to himself: 'I think that water butt sticks out too far into the path; it would be better round the corner,' and so it was moved out of position.

This is a sad picture of a good many Christian lives today – they are out of position, out of touch. For the sake of this world, with all its need, let us get into position, into touch with Christ. Let there be perfect fellowship, and then His grace will flow into our life, and we shall have 'all sufficiency'.

'ASK & YOU SHALL RECEIVE':

Sometime ago I had a letter from a poor fellow who was down and out. He was a Colonial, and had come over to this country a few years back. He had a good job in an office, but the Hatry crash came, his firm wound up, and eventually he found himself on the streets. He had spent his savings, and had come to the end of everything, when he wrote me a pitiful letter. He began by telling me why he was addressing me. He wrote: 'I am quite unknown to you, but in my despair I walked across Hyde Park, and as I sat down on a seat, I wondered what to do next. There was a lady sitting next to me. I told her a bit of my story (I do not know who she was), and when I had finished, she said to me: "What you want to do is to write to Lindsay Glegg," and she handed me your name and address written on a sheet of paper. Hence I am sending you this letter.'

I felt that the letter had a true ring about it. I thought to myself somehow or other, God has brought together two people, both unknown to me, and one has influenced the other to write to me. I think I can see God's hand in this. I knew I had a very busy day ahead of me, but before I started out I felt I must write him a line, and so I dropped him a note. I said: 'I will help you. I can get you the medical attention you need. Here is a one pound Treasury Note to see you through the week-end. Write me again and keep in touch with me.'

I posted the letter. After ten days the envelope came back. Everything in it was intact, the Treasury Note inside, and my own letter, and on the outside of the envelope was written the words, 'Left, present address unknown.' I thought to myself: 'What a pity he did not trust me!' He sent out his cry; he sent out his S.O.S. and he never waited for the answer! I suppose he said to himself: 'I have written hundreds of letters. This is only another one but it is no good. I will never get an answer. It is not worth waiting for a reply.' For all I know he ended his days as he intended doing, in the Thames. What a pity he did not trust me!

We would not treat our Lord like that. He has got all the riches of heaven for us. We are paupers, but we have a friend who never fails, and who is rich beyond all reckoning. We may come to Him, asking from Him until we are filled, for there is no stint in His giving.

CHRIST'S EVER-OPEN HANDS:

A friend of mine was shown over a great locomotive works in one of our industrial towns in Britain. The manager showed him everything. He was taken through the drawing office, and into the pattern shop; he was shown over the foundry, where the great castings were made, and then on to the machine shop. Next, they went into the fitting and erecting sheds and, finally, into the great testing department where the big locomotives were tested out before they were sent out on service. And when my friend returned to the office again, he stretched out his hand, and thanked the manager for all he had done. Gripping the manager's hand, he found it did not respond to a warm handshake, so he quickly let go of the manager's hand. He saw at once that he had done wrong; for the manager coloured up for a moment, and then he said to my friend, 'Sir, you must excuse my hand. When I was an apprentice I met with an accident, and a nail was driven through my hand, and I have never been able to close it since.' My friend said, 'May I shake hands with you again?' and as he held the hand of that manager, he said, 'May I tell you something? Nearly two thousand years ago there was One who left the glory of Heaven, and came down as a child to live on this earth: and He went about doing good. But they took Him and drove the nails through His hands, for they nailed Him to a Cross; and He died there for our sins that we might be forgiven. He died that we might be set free from the thraldom of sin. And I want to tell you that He has never closed His hand since. His are ever-open hands.'

THE OLD GOLF PUTTER:

One day two men walked down a garden path and they talked together as they went. When they got to the end of the garden they stood opposite an old shed; there were a lot of garden implements in it, old boxes, a few spades, a good deal of rubbish and litter. And as they talked together one man said to the other, 'What is that you have got on the shelf there?' 'Why, it's an old golf club,' replied the other, and he took down from the shelf an old, rusty, disused, dusty putter. The other swung it in his hand, and he said to his friend, 'I like the feel of this club; I like the balance of it, do you mind if I have it?' 'Take it away,' said his friend, 'I can do no good with it. I threw it in there one day in despair, and it has been on this shelf ever since.' That night the man went on his homeward way with this old, rusty, discarded putter under his arm. Some time after that at St. Andrew's Golf Course the ball was hit on the eighteenth green, and travelling across the green the ball fell into the hole – that putt will be remembered as long as the game of golf lasts, for by that shot Bobby Jones won the Open Championship of Great Britain.

In the same year he won the Amateur Championship of Great Britain. And in the same year he won the Open and the Amateur Championships of the United States of America – all the four events in one year. Such a thing had never been done before, and I do not suppose it will ever be done again. But Bobby Jones did it, and he did it with that old rusty, disused, castaway putter. As all the world knows, that putter is now historic. It goes by the name of 'Calamity Jane'. I read in the newspaper not very long ago that Bobby Jones was going out once again to play, and he was taking 'Calamity Jane' with him. That disused, rusty putter once on the shelf, yes, but now in the hands of a great master, who carried it from victory to victory.

Will you put your life into the hands of Christ today? Some of you, although you are quite young, are beginning to realise that your lives have already got rusty and aimless; you feel you are on the shelf, and the dust of the world has gathered round you. Some of you young people are dissatisfied; your aims and your ambitions are

not being fulfilled, and you are discontented, but you are
in earnest. I have got a word for you. If you will put your
life into the hands of Christ, He will lay hold of you, He
will take you into that eternal hand of His, that hand that
was nailed to the Cross for you, that hand that has never
lost a single soul yet, that hand which will lay hold of you,
and carry you right up the steep hills of life, through all
the storms, and through whatever experiences may lie
before you. He will hold on to you, and keep you to the
end.

'LORD, TAKE MY LIFE'

Some time ago I had an intimation that the site on which
my works were built would be required, and that Parlia-
mentary powers had been given to take the site over from
me. A consulting engineer came down in order to assess
the value of the works that were going to be comman-
deered, and I took him round my place, and tried to make
the best of the situation. I showed him the buildings, and
said, 'The roof wants patching up a bit; a little paint here
and there will do no harm; a pane or two of glass might
be put in. I can have all that done for you.' And I told the
best story I could.

He said to me, 'Mr Glegg, may I have a word with
you in your office?' We went in together, and he said, 'I
want to be quite frank with you. I do not want your
buildings, for the whole of this place is going to be levelled
to the ground. What we want is the *site*, and on this spot
we are going to erect a great power station which is to
send electricity out into the villages and the cities of the
south-east of England. Away, over in Guildford, there
will be a light shining that is fed from this place. Away
yonder, right down to Dover, they will draw their power
from here. We want the situation.' What does the Lord
require of us? Our patched-up lives? – 'I will make things
a little better'; 'I will try to adjust things': 'I will be a

little more careful'. 'I must make a few good resolutions';
'There are certain things I must attend to.'

No. God wants the situation, the vantage ground of
your life. Will you lay your life at His feet? Will you give
Him that broken life of yours which has been a dis-
appointment to you? Will you hand that life over to the
Lord Jesus, and say, 'Lord, take me; I will renounce
everything and follow Thee'? What will it mean? It will
mean that in whatever part of the world we live there will
be a light shining. Away in Glasgow there will be a power
centre, because someone there is following Christ. Over
yonder in London there will be a light shining that will
become a beacon guide to others. Because the Lord Jesus
has been given the situation, from which He can radiate
His power and glory. Will you give Him the situation?
Will you yield your life to Him?

KESWICK CONVENTION:

There are some meetings that seem to find a lasting place
in our memories. I can remember listening, as a boy, to
Signor Marconi giving his first lecture in England at the
Royal Institution. In my mind's eye I can see him now
as he stood facing a distinguished audience of scientists,
describing to them the wonders of the wireless. It was an
historic occasion when, in a silence that could be felt, a
message was passed from one gallery to another without
the use of wires. Those that understood the Morse Code
recognised the message, which was 'God save the Queen',
and that great audience rose to its feet and cheered again
and again.

Only a few weeks ago I was at another memorable
meeting, when Madame Joliot Curie spoke of the latest
discoveries in connection with Radium. And who among
those who were privileged to be present at the funeral of
our late beloved King will ever forget that solemn and
sacred occasion?

But I venture to suggest that the gathering that faces me now in this huge tent at the Keswick Convention in 1936, is in some respects the most remarkable of all. Why have thousands of people from many parts of the world gathered here? Is it merely for a holiday? Is it simply to meet friends? To view the beautiful scenery? To row across the lake or climb the mountains? None of these things will account for this great audience. This eager throng has gathered to meet with God. Men and women hungering and thirsting after righteousness, have come here to be satisfied.

THE WORLD'S NEED:

I was in Scotland a little while ago. As I had an hour or two to wait for my train coming south, the director of a firm who was with me said, 'I would like you to see our picture gallery: it has only recently been opened, and we have some fine pictures.' I went round this picture gallery, and I looked at the pictures. One I looked at in passing was a painting of still life. There was some fruit on the table, beside a jug, a curtain behind, and a tablecloth in front. I glanced at it, and I thought to myself. 'Well that's a bit of a daub!' I was about to pass on, when the Curator of the picture gallery touched me on the shoulder and said: 'Mr Glegg, what do you think of that picture?' Well, it was rather an awkward question, and not having anything very brilliant to say, I said nothing (I believe that is a wise policy. We would often be thought much wiser than we are, if we did not talk so much). I knew he wanted to say something, and I was right, for he gave me ten minutes of that picture. 'Why,' he said, 'it is surely not painted on a flat piece of canvas. Look how it recedes. Look at the depth in it. Look at the light and shade. Look at the bloom on the fruit. Look at the balance of the picture, see how it all heads up to one point.' As he began to describe the picture, my casual glance become a vision. The picture began to grip me. I saw things in it that I had not seen before. I saw something of what was in the artist's mind, and how he had been able to place it on the canvas. I have now in my mind's eye a vivid memory of that picture. A casual glance became a vision. Has the world's need, the need of the people at home, in the office, in our circle of friends – has it become a vision that has gripped you? We shall never move the world for God till we are mastered by the vision of the world's need.

Extracts from an Interview with
Mr A. Lindsay Glegg on his 90th birthday

JLF: Mr. Glegg, with a life spanning 90 years as Pastor, Evangelist, Golfer, Author, Gardener and Counsellor. I find it difficult to know where to begin. You were saying that you find it easier to recollect events of 70 years ago, than something which took place 7 days ago. Can you recall something of the reign of Queen Victoria?

ALG: I was always fascinated by Queen Victoria, because my mother was at school with Queen Victoria's housekeeper at Balmoral. In my early days I used to wander all over Balmoral Castle, even into the Queen's bedroom when she wasn't there. When she arrived I was hustled out. I saw a good deal of the Queen in those early days. I remember as a little boy of 7 or 8, playing alone on the bank of a road near Balmoral when, lo and behold, the Queen drove up with the Princess in a carriage and pair, with her two Indian attendants sitting behind her. I was astute enough to recognise Her Majesty and I took my little school cap off and the Queen smiled at me and the Princess kissed her hand at me - so you see I'm a very important person – no Princess kissed her hand at you! I was at the Queen's diamond jubilee and also at her funeral. There I saw about 40 European Kings, including the Kaiser, but they've nearly all lost their heads or gone. Of course, that was a much more leisurely age than now – we had plenty of domestic help; there were no motor cars; there were no saxophones – they weren't invented. We had no entertainment and therefore we had to amuse ourselves, and the only place where we could get any fellowship was at church and that's where we had social evenings. If we invited each other to our own homes then we had to amuse ourselves with charades, somebody playing the piano or singing – we all had to do something and we could do in those days because every girl in a middle-class family learned to play the piano or the violin – it was the natural thing to do. Of course, girls stayed at home; it was the First World War that brought the girls into the offices and created afternoon tea, which nobody had heard of before.

JLF: I understand that you came into blessing in 1905 as a result of the Welsh Revival spreading across to the Keswick Convention. Some historians are now asserting that this was not a genuine awakening.

ALG: Well, there's no doubt that it was a genuine awakening and that people were turned from drunkenness to sobriety. About a quarter of a million people were added to the Church membership and I've met many of them and they were still rejoicing and glorying in the Welsh Revival. Certainly my experience of it was that the power of God came down and took over and people were stricken down with repentance and it was there that I saw reality. Before that I had been subject to the 'new theology' which was brought in by R. J. Campbell, and that meant that I had been carried out into the wilderness and the Bible was very largely treated as stories and myth.

JLF: Your first wife had close family associations with C. H. Spurgeon. Did she ever speak of her memories of the great preacher?

ALG: Oh yes she did, because Spurgeon always went for tea, at her parents house in Wandsworth, on Sunday afternoons. Spurgeon used to take her on his knee and told her stories at tea-time and then she remembers him taking an old envelope out of his pocket and writing down on the back of it his subject for the sermon – he wrote down three or four headings, out of his mind, and that was his sermon for that night.

JLF: Speaking of another great preacher, it's very interesting to me that you knew Gypsy Smith, as a friend, because I look on him as one of the almost legendary figures in the history of evangelism.

ALG: Yes, he was a great soul and I had a great admiration for him. He had a wonderful flow of language, that, for a gypsy boy, was truly remarkable – beautiful language - and then he could make you laugh and after weeping and laughing he could do what he liked with you ! When he gave the appeal you were bound to come out. In those days evangelists gave straight-forward messages – if you had a miniature Sankey with you, as the brothers Wood did, that helped. Otherwise you had to preach a straight forward gospel message and then make your appeal followed by an after-meeting, which was really the vital thing. The appeal was essential in order that you might get the folks who were really anxious and who wanted to come to the Saviour.

JLF: I understand that you learned a great deal from Lionel Fletcher on the subject of drawing in the gospel net?

ALG: Lionel Fletcher used to say – 'They must do something about it; if you let your congregation go away without a challenge and without giving them a chance to respond you've lost them psychologically as well as spiritually. I don't mind if they come out or put up their hands. I don't mind how they do it but they've got to do something, even if it means crossing their fingers under the pew. Having done something, they've said this is a sign, those crossed fingers – nobody knows but I know - that is the sign that I have given my life to Christ.' The importance of that is rather forgotten. It's the easiest thing to let your crowd go away with everyone saying – 'that was a good sermon and

I'm sure there were a lot of people blessed' but when you make an appeal you take your reputation into your own hands because it requires courage and if no-one comes forward it's difficult for evangelists to take a blow like that. I believe that is the reason why some evangelists are tempted to forsake their true calling and become Bible teachers because they are afraid their reputations would suffer if there is no response to their appeal for people to receive Christ.

JLF: Your books are liberally sprinkled with fascinating biographical sketches of Bible characters. Do you have one particular favourite?

ALG: Well, I'm afraid Paul is my hero because I so built myself up on Romans and the other epistles of Paul. I learnt doctrine there and I learnt the meaning of the Cross and the Resurrection and also the coming again of our Lord. I don't always hear that note of the crucified Christ and what actually happened on the Cross when He died. That has always been the basis of my own assurance that I was grounded in the faith through Paul, although, of course, the other characters in the Bible are wonderful too.

JLF: Apart from your development of the young people's meetings at Keswick and the establishment of the Filey Christian Holiday Crusade, what are the things that you would really like to be remembered for?

ALG: If I could be thought of as one who showed forth the fruits of the Spirit. I think one's own life has a great deal to do with one's ministry. If your life rings true you'll not only enjoy your ministry but it will be blessed. If your life isn't perfectly adjusted to the Will of God, you'll find preaching is a hard job and you won't get much enjoyment out of it. One of my favourite texts is – 'He that abideth in Me, and I in him, the same bringeth forth much fruit' – so there's the condition and there's the result.

JLF: During your many travels you must have stayed in homes where the hostess enquired whether you had any dislikes as far as food is concerned. How did you reply?

ALG: Oh I generally say, 'If you really want to know, there are three things I don't like – they are liver, kidneys and hypocrisy!'

JLF: Mr Glegg, most of your contemporaries are now 'with Christ'. How do you view the prospect of joining them?

ALG: Nearly all of my contemporaries have gone – raced me to glory. I've had such a lot to thank God for – for, at least, 70 years of serving

Him and for the lovely opportunities He has given me – far more than I ever deserved but I rejoice in that and I shall be very happy when the time comes to go. I'm not looking forward to dying because nobody likes the fact of dying – it's quite an ordeal with all the people gathering around you and the nurse feels your pulse and say's, 'well, it won't be long now' and they don't think you hear it but you hear all the comments and I don't think dying is at all a good thing to look forward to, but death is. I would just like to go when the Lord has finished with me down here and then I'll be delighted to go to glory. I'm just very happy at present in being able to serve Him.